CANAL BOATMAN

A YORK STATE BOOK

A single canal boat and team moving westward through the Lockport rock cut. Photo *circa* 1870s.

CANAL BOATMAN

My Life on Upstate Waterways

RICHARD GARRITY

SYRACUSE UNIVERSITY PRESS

The paper used in this publication meets the minimum requirements of American National Standard for Information Sciences—Permanence of Paper for Printed Library Materials, ANSI Z39.48. ∞™

Library of Congress Cataloging in Publication Data

Garrity, Richard G.
  Canal boatman.

  (A York State book)
  1. Garrity, Richard G   2. Boatmen—New York (State)
—Biography.   3. Canals—New York (State)—History.
I. Title.
HE569.G37A32   386'.4042'40924   [B]   77-21909
ISBN 0-8156-0191-3/GACBP

Manufactured in the United States of America

Foreword

THIS BOOK, the author has said, was written "mainly because it brought back to me a fascinating and happy boyhood spent on the Erie Canal." He worked on the manuscript of "Canal Boatman" for almost six years, and it is a personal memoir of valuable Americana. He has drawn upon contacts and interviews with men like himself who also spent their boyhood on the old Erie Canal and then worked the Barge Canal in later years; but his main source has been himself—his own record and memories of those times and conditions when he was a young boy aboard his father's canal boats and, later, as a husband and father striving to raise a family, working the Barge Canal and other waterways.

The author of "Recollections of the Erie Canal," a booklet published by the Historical Society of the Tonawandas, of which he is a charter member, he also provided some material used in George R. Condon's *Stars in the Water,* a Cleveland journalist's book on the Erie Canal published in 1974.

When Richard G. Garrity was born, his father was managing the former Bork Hotel in Tonawanda. From 1905 until 1916, when his father operated two canal boats first in the lumber trade and later for gravel hauling, the author was growing up surrounded by the busy and fascinating life of a now bygone era in canal boating in upstate New York. His father had begun canalling as an Erie Canal boathand in 1880, and he drove mules and horses on all the towpaths of that waterway between Albany and Buffalo. From the time that he was a small lad, the author spent every season on the canal from 1905 until it was abandoned at the end of the 1917 season when the Barge Canal System took over.

This book contains a large and intriguing sampling of little-known history and the lore of canal boating, and of the men who worked the Barge Canal and the Erie before it. Fascinating incidental information appears in almost every chapter—anecdotes of animal-powered old canal boats, as well as the later diesel-powered tugs; comments on the celebrated canal-boat mules and the drivers and steersmen who tended them; recollections of the farmers and grocers along the towpath; and descriptive definitions of many canal-related terms that comprised the common vocabulary of boaters in the early 1900s. Richard Garrity discusses the nature of virtually all types of work connected with canalling and the equipment used, and offers insight into many aspects of family life aboard a canal boat. He has gone beyond the half-fact, half-fiction of works like Sam Adams' *Grandfather Stories* and such other books dealing with the canal days to provide an authentic picture of what canal boating was really like.

CANAL COMPARISONS

	The Erie or Grand Canal	Enlarged Erie Canal	Barge Canal—Erie Section
Length	363 miles	350.5 miles	340.7 miles
Number of locks	83	72	35
Size of canal (prism)	40 x 26 x 4 ft	70 x 52-56 x 7 ft	Earth sections: 123 x 75 x 12* Rock sections: 94 ft wide River sections: 200 ft wide
Size of locks	15 x 90 ft (4 ft of water over miter sills)	18 x 110 ft (7 ft of water over miter sills)	44.5 x 300 ft
Size of boats	14 x 75 ft 75 tons capacity 3.5 ft draft	16 x 96 ft 240-250 tons capacity	2000 tons (original vessel capacity) 10 ft draft*
Clearance under bridges		11 ft	15.5 ft*

*Except from Hudson River to Oswego, depth has been increased to 14 ft (boat draft 12 ft) and bridge clearance to 20 ft.

Note: The Champlain, Oswego and Cayuga-Seneca branch canals have the same dimensions as the Erie Division of the Barge Canal, except for the changes made between the Hudson River and Oswego.

This book is furthermore—and importantly—the narrative of a canaller eking a living for himself and his family in the 1920s and the Depression thirties, working during the boating season on the canal and taking various jobs "ashore" during the winter months and at other times when canal work was slow or unobtainable; but like fictional characters in an Edmonds novel, he always seemed more content when he was working on the canal. In the early 1940s he obtained steady employment with the Great Lakes Towing Company in Buffalo—"in the line of work I like best," he said. That job lasted twenty-seven years, until he retired at the end of the 1970 season.

Here is that rarity in publishing: a manuscript chock full of Americana that is not only significant but interestingly written—a book by an author whose life and work have been intimately bound up with the famed Big Ditch which has been referred to in more romantic literature as "the shining ribbon of water." There are few other books like this one about any of the canals, and none so complete by a person who has lived and worked on the waterways of upstate New York.

Cumberland, Rhode Island   Lionel D. Wyld

Preface

I AM a charter-member of the Historical Society of the Tonawandas, Inc., which was formed in 1960. Tonawanda is a canal town, and when canal questions came up I was the member best informed to answer them. I was urged by the Society's President, Willard Dittmar, to do some writing about the canal. I was not too keen about the idea, as I had never written anything longer than a letter. After thinking it over for a while, I felt that my background and experience gave me a wide range of knowledge on canals and other waterways that had not been written about by anyone who had spent his boyhood on Erie Canal boats and later earned his living on the waterways of his native New York State.

I wrote the first booklet of 36 pages which was published by the Society in 1966. It was well received locally, and the 1000 copies were soon sold out. Later on, the booklet was enlarged and reprinted. I received many favorable comments on the enlarged booklet and realized that I had only scratched the surface on what I could write about. That was when I began to write this book, and I enjoyed it, for it brought back many boyhood memories and recollections of all the boatmen I had known through the years.

I did not go back to school at the end of the summer I became fourteen. My reasons were practical ones: I wanted to keep on being a boatman, and I also wanted to keep on working to help out with the family finances. I was at that time the second oldest of nine children and I knew we were deeply in debt. When I told my father that I wanted to quit school, he did not object too much but told me I would be sorry later on. I said to myself, "I can read, write and figure—what more schooling do I need?" Who knows about these things? Had I gone to school longer, I may have taken up some other kind of work and would not have acquired the boating experience and knowledge to write this book.

I am deeply grateful for the help and encouragement of the many friends and acquaintances who aided me in various ways, either academically or technically. Particularly, I would like to express my thanks and appreciation to Robert H. Lloyd; Evelyn Schlicher; and Willard Dittmar, director of the Historical Society of the Tonawandas, Inc.; Mrs. Clyde Helfer, iconologist of the Buffalo and Erie County Historical Society; Shirley Stowater and Williams Loos, the rare book room curator of the Buffalo and Erie County Public Library; Mrs. Buford Bellinger and William Kibler of the Tonawanda Public Library; the Canal Society of New York State at Syracuse; and Charles Boyer, curator of the Niagara County Historical Society at Lockport. A very special thanks goes to Virginia Vidler, author and writer of East Aurora, N.Y., for steering a very inexperienced author into the right channels for getting his efforts published; and to Carolyn Sexton and Vivian Cole of Hamburg, N.Y., for being "on deck" to help with a breakdown in operations at a critical time. Also many thanks are extended to Howard J. Finley, director of the Old Brutus Historical Society, for his answer to my letter of inquiry regarding an event that took place at Weedsport a long time ago; to Captain Archy Thurston for corroborating my remembrances of places, times, and things; and to Captain Frank H. Godfrey for the same reasons and for the material he contributed to aid me in some of the Barge Canal sections of the book.

To my wife Mildred for her help and encouragement in seeing this book through to the finish I owe a special debt, which I am especially happy to acknowledge here.

Tonawanda, New York   Richard Garrity
Spring 1977

Contents

CANAL BOATMAN

CHAPTER 1

Family History and Canal Boats

I N THE EARLY 1900s our family became the owners of a pair of Erie Canal lumber boats and two teams of mules. The boats carried lumber to Albany and New York City. I spent every season on the canal from the time I was two years old in 1905 until it was abandoned at the end of the 1917 canal season. The route of the canal through the cities and towns of New York State and the numerous historic sites visible from it, plus the many family discussions and boyhood memories of the canal, have kept it fresh in my mind.

My father, Richard J. Garrity, was born July 6, 1867, at Liverpool, New York, a village on the outskirts of Syracuse. He was the youngest of four children and often mentioned that his parents came to America from County Cork, Ireland. There were no relatives in this country.

When Richard was seven, his fifteen-year-old brother, James, died an accidental death caused from being kicked in the head by a horse. His mother's death occurred a short time after the death of her oldest child. Father believed that the tragic accident, added to other misfortunes, contributed to the untimely death of his mother, Bridget Garrity. Soon after his mother passed away, he was placed in a nearby orphanage.

His sister Margaret was taken in and raised by a local family. She eventually married and lived out her life in Syracuse. His older brother, John, who was thirteen when the family broke up, went

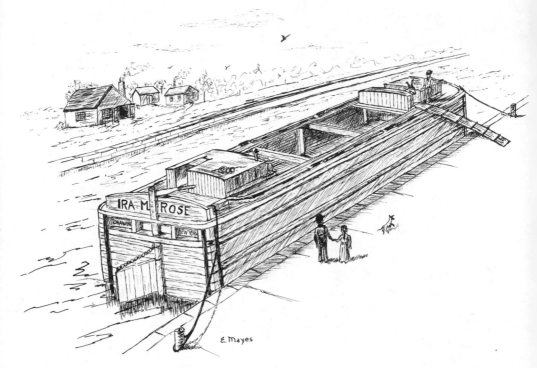

An empty lumber boat. Many Erie Canal boats of this type were built at various boatyards in Tonawanda, N.Y., until 1912. A few grain-carrying steam canal fleets were built afterwards. The opening of the new Barge Canal was then but a short time away, and the year 1915 saw the closing of the last Tonawanda boatyard. Drawing by E. Mayes.

to work on the Erie Canal. What became of his father, James Garrity, who had placed him in the orphanage, was never known, and he seldom spoke of him.

My father may have been embittered by his own father's indifference; however, when he became a parent of thirteen children, he looked after them, and had the respect and affection of all of his family. He never missed an opportunity to attend church, and gave us a mild lecture when we did not follow his example. He devoted all his efforts to his family, and was always in debt from just ordinary living expenses, until most of us were able to look out for ourselves. Although never too successful financially, he was always trying, and enjoyed a modest security for twenty-one years after retiring at the age of seventy.

To get back to father's boyhood, at the age of nine he was released from the orphanage to an elderly farm couple, who wanted a youngster for company and to help out around the farm. He spent the next three years on the farm near Liverpool, New York, which he always called his hometown. While living on the farm, he took care of the light chores about the place and was clothed and fed and had some schooling during the winter months. Well treated by the couple who made a home for him, he always spoke kindly of them in later years.

When Richard became twelve the elderly farm couple decided to sell out and retire. By this time his brother John, now seventeen, was operating a boat on the Erie Canal. John had been keeping in touch with his younger brother through the years, and was notified of the intended retirement. It was a happy day for young Richard when his brother came to take him from the farm. In the spring of 1880 he became a canaller working alongside his brother.

I recall that father had a deep affection for my Uncle John and was always happy to see him in later years. John Garrity had retired from the canal and was operating a canalside farm near Poorhouse Lock, a mile or so west of Lyons, New York, when he died of pneumonia in April of 1912 at the age of fifty. He was buried in Tonawanda; the funeral was conducted from our home.

Spending his early life on the canal, Father drove mules on all the towpaths of the New York State canal system. Bound from Syracuse to Philadelphia on a canal boat loaded with salt, the fifteen-year-old boatman passed under the Brooklyn Bridge on the day it opened, May 24, 1883. The opening date was also Queen Victoria's birthday. Father always remembered the day and the date.

Spending one winter in an Adirondack lumber camp as a roustabout, Father told of arising at four in the morning to start the fires in the bunkhouse and in the kitchen for the cook to prepare breakfast for the lumberjacks. Among other things, he peeled potatoes and vegetables, washed dishes, set tables, swept the floor, and made himself generally useful. He would take any kind of work that was available when the canal was closed. Some winters he drove a team of horses on construction jobs in Syracuse.

When asked if he had many fights while driving on the canal, he mentioned only one, with another young driver. Winning this fight, he never mentioned any others.

By the 1880s the rough and tumble day on the canal had quieted down. Many of the canal fleets were owned and operated by sober, responsible men, who made a comfortable home on the boats for their families during the canal season.

Father first learned about life on the canal as a driver, and he later became a steersman. Still later, he ran and managed boats for owners who chose to stay home and hire a competent man to run them as an investment.

When thirty-three years old he left the canal for a few years and managed the Bork Hotel from 1900 to 1904. It was located on North Niagara Street, facing the canal in Tonawanda, New York. The hotel was patronized by lake sailors and canal men. Here he met my mother, Wilhelmina Kohler, who was working there at the time. They were married November 7, 1900, and often spoke of attending the Pan American Exposition held in Buffalo in 1901; this was about the nearest they came to having a honeymoon. My brother James was born in the hotel in 1901, and I was born there on August 11, 1903.

The Erie Canal played a part in the early life of my mother's family. She never talked very much about her girlhood, for she became fatherless at the age of eleven, and from then on she had little time for play or social life. Her brother, my Uncle Charles, who had driven mules for several seasons on the canal for my father, told me some of the family history that he recalled from his early boyhood.

Their father, Jacob Kohler, and his brother, Henry, ran a clothing store in Tonawanda from 1880 to 1891. Kohler Brothers' Store was on North Canal Street (now North Niagara Street) near the Tonawanda sidecut lock.

A large part of the store's business was done with lake sailors and canallers. Uncle Charles told me of an incident regarding the store that he had never forgotten. It concerned a one-legged canal driver. I had seen drivers with one arm or one eye, and other handicaps, but had never known a driver with a peg leg. How he managed to walk an average of ten or twelve miles every other six hours along the towpath is a mystery to me.

The Bork Hotel, Tonawanda, N.Y., was built in 1880 on North Canal Street. The iron railing in the foreground separated the street from the heelpath of the Erie Canal. The author was born on the second floor on August 11, 1903. Notice how the veranda posts are chewed away while faithful old Dobbin waited for his master to cease bending his elbow at the bar. Most of the men in the picture are wearing white shirts, so the picture must have been taken on a Sunday. Photo 1892.

Erie Canal and towpath on the left, in the heart of the Tonawandas business district. Two animal-towed Erie Canal lumber boats are shown ready to start down the canal. Photo *circa* spring 1898.

This driver stopped in the store one day as his boats were passing through the lock, on the way to load lumber at the docks along the Niagara River. Ordering a pair of trousers from Henry Kohler, he requested that one pant leg be cut off to the proper length for his peg leg. He then asked if they could be ready when the loaded boats came back through the lock, as they would continue right on down the canal. The pants were ready on time, the driver stopped in the store, picked them up and went aboard the boats which were soon on their way east.

After arriving at Albany, the peg leg driver decided to put on his new pair of pants purchased at the Kohler Brothers and go uptown. When he tried to put them on, he found that the wrong leg of the trousers had been cut off! Knowing canal men, he must have let out a few choice cuss words, which expressed his feelings in rather harsh terms.

He made his displeasure known to the Kohler Brothers at the first opportunity on his return to Tonawanda. The story was soon known all over town and probably traveled the length of the canal. No doubt it brought a smile to the face of many a canaller, as it did to ours, when my uncle related the incident to me.

Asking if it was this type of customer service that caused my grandfather and his brother to give up the clothing store in 1891,

Tonawanda's Erie Canal Spillway adjoined the Niagara River on the western side of the city. It was built to help relieve the spring flood waters of Tonawanda Creek. Photo *circa* 1920.

I was told that the business failure was caused by too much credit to lake sailors and to canal men who never returned to pay their bills.

Another reason for the failure involved my great Uncle Henry, who was an ardent fisherman. When his brother Jacob had to be absent from the store on business trips or for other reasons, Henry would close the store, or fail to open it at all, and go fishing. Henry was more devoted to fishing than he was to any type of business, and he remained that way until the end of his days.

Soon after closing the store, Grandfather Jacob Kohler entered a new field, the amusement business. He bought a canal boat that was housed over from end to end, which was fitted out to carry a knocked down or portable merry-go-round. This he set up in various towns along the canal between Buffalo and Rochester in the year 1892. The next year he boated the merry-go-round to Rochester, and had it hauled by teams to the amusement park at Seabreeze, on Lake Ontario, a few miles east of Rochester, where it was set up for the season.

He died an accidental death at Seabreeze, and there was something of a mystery surrounding his death at the age of thirty-five. Near evening he had told his fellow workers that he was going to clean up and go home a few days to visit his family in Tonawanda. The next day he was found dead at the bottom of a deep gully or ravine near the edge of the amusement park. It was assumed that before leaving for home he had started down the steep incline leading to the bottom of the gully, which contained a spring used for drinking and washing, and that while making the descent, he had slipped and tumbled to the bottom. Being a heavy-built man, he had ruptured a blood vessel in his leg. His death being caused by an internal injury, the authorities ruled it as accidental.

Grandfather was known to carry considerable sums of money, but none was found on his body. Having no money in his possession, being in debt because of his business, his death left his wife and four young children destitute.

To the end of her days my grandmother was suspicious that foul play was the cause of her husband's death, because she knew that he always carried a good sum of money on his person. She did not believe that someone could have found the body, removed the money, and failed to notify the police of the accident.

My mother was the oldest of four children. Grandmother kept the family together by conducting a hand laundry in her home. Mother had to take over most of the housework, and the three younger boys picked up and delivered the laundry. Grandmother supported her four children in this manner until they grew up and were able to take care of her and themselves.

Mother recalled the house rent was six dollars a month. The only help the family received was a dollar and a half weekly grocery order from the Commissioner of the Poor. My Uncle Charles remembered that "the grocery order contained plenty of baloney."

If the reader reflects on my parents' family history, he can only conclude that they never enjoyed the carefree childhood which they provided for me.

Feeling that he was not cut out for the hotel business, Father gave up the managing job and returned to the calling he liked best, that of being a canaller. He bought a pair of used lumber boats, in good condition, in 1905, and took his family with him on the boats; that was the start of my canal days.

The boats were named the *Martin Hyde* and the *Sol Gold-smith.* We never knew for whom the *Martin Hyde* was named, but the *Sol Goldsmith* was named after a local clothing store owner in North Tonawanda.

The average individual boat owner at that time had two boats. These were usually bought with a down payment and a mortgage on the boats for the balance of the payment, which was paid out of the boat's earnings. He also had to have six head of stock (mules or horses), collars, harnesses, whiffletrees, and other necessary trappings. Hiring competent and reliable drivers and steersmen was another of his problems. He also had to arrange with brokers for cargoes and cargo insurance.

The boat owner's credit had to be good with drydock owners and canal boat suppliers. At the end of the season, he arranged for the boarding of the mules with a nearby farmer. During the winter months the boats had to be kept pumped out and the boat's equipment looked after, so that it was not stolen before spring came around.

A canal boat owner was occasionally subjected to costly re-pair bills for damages to the boats caused by striking objects in the canal or by having the cabins torn off by hitting low bridges when the boats were light. He could also suffer the loss of his mules such as my father did in the Rock Cut above Lockport.

Once, with our two boats loaded with lumber for Albany, we had left Tonawanda before dark on a summer evening. So when I went to bed I thought we would be below Lockport and on our way over the upper long level when I got up for breakfast. When Mother called me the next morning, I was surprised to find out that we were still above the Lockport locks. She did not seem to be her usual cheerful self, and I sensed that something had gone wrong. On inquiring, I was told that our team of mules had fallen into the canal and had drowned a mile or so above the locks. The current had carried the boats along and we were lying tied up at the head of the locks. Nearby, I could see the two drowned mules floating in the canal with their collars and harnesses still on. The current also had carried them down to the locks during the night. The driver was safe, but I could sense the general air of gloom that was felt by everyone on the boats.

When I asked how it happened, I was told that the wind had

A single canal boat and team moving westward through the Lockport rock cut. The planks on the towpath just ahead of the team on the left cover an animal escape hole. The opening in the canal wall at right of the escape hole is the entrance. The opening in the towpath at the left end of planks is the ramp which allowed a mule to get back on the towpath. The picture was taken from Hitchings Bridge about 1½ miles east of the locks. The escape hole can still be seen from the new bridge, but it is now filled with concrete. Photo *circa* 1870s.

picked up during the night, and a sudden gust had blown a piece of paper along the towpath toward the mules. This caused the inside mule to shy and crowd the other mule off the towpath into the canal. As they were hitched together, one mule had pulled the other into the water with him. The towpath in the Rock Cut at this point was six or seven feet above the water's edge, and the night being very dark, the mules soon became entangled in their harnesses and drowned. Had it been daylight they might have been saved.

In some sections of the canal, especially through the Rock Cut and cities where the canal sides were walled or built straight up and down, escape holes were provided in the canal walls to save the animals from being drowned, should they accidentally fall in the water. The escape hole was an opening cut across and below the towpath down to or below the water's edge. The opening in the towpath was planked over, and a ramp was provided so that the animals could be led back up to the side of the towpath.

There were a number of escape holes in the three-mile-long Rock Cut west of Lockport. The old Erie Canal towpath, now overgrown with weeds and brush, is still in the original cut. Mules were still being used for towing when this section of the old Erie was enlarged to Barge Canal dimensions, since only rock from the south side of the cut was removed for the conversion.

In this particular place along the towpath, however, nothing could have been done to save our two mules in the darkness. They had been an exceptionally fine span. Both were young and strong, big and heavy. Father had said that they were able to do the work of three ordinary mules. He had paid a high price for them that spring and felt very badly about losing them.

It had been a tragic incident and a financial setback, not soon forgotten. We stayed in Lockport a few more hours until the mules were replaced. The drowned mules were pulled from the canal; the harnesses were removed, and the carcasses hauled off to a rendering plant.

To me, a very young boy, the drowning of the team was a most sad event. Because of the financial worries, a pall had settled over my parents, which took many days for time to erase. The incident happened about 1907 or 1908 and was the only time any loss of mules occurred during the time we owned the boats.

When the canal opened for the season of 1905 we were a family of five—my parents, my brother James (a year and a half older than I), a younger sister, Margaret, and I. Mother and we children returned each spring to the canal boats with father. We would leave Tonawanda about May 15 and return with the boats not later than mid-November.

The canal season of 1914 was the last that Mother and all

Open view of an animal escape hole which was built to retrieve animals that had fallen into the canal from the towpath. There were a number of these holes in the three-mile-long rock cut above Lockport, where the canal sides were walled straight up and down. They were also provided in towns and cities along the canal that had laid up stone walls. Drawing by E. Mayes.

the family were to be on the boats with Father during the canal season. There were then seven children living with Mother and Father in the small living space of a canal boat cabin, the youngest a babe in arms, the next a toddler. The older children missed many days of school during the canal season. There was also the worry of accidents or the drowning of one of the children. There was not enough room on a canal boat for so large a family. It is hard for me to realize how my mother coped with raising her family on a canal boat as long as she did. When we were boating lumber she cooked for two drivers, a steersman, and her own family, which was smaller at that time. When boating gravel there was only a steersman and our family, which by then was much larger. In 1914, the last year she was on the boat, she cooked for the steersman, Father, herself, and seven children. The table had to be set and cleared off twice; there was not room enough for everyone to eat at the same time. The dishes were washed in a dishpan on the cleared-off table. The water for laundering the clothes had to be dipped up from the canal and heated on the woodburning stove in a copper wash boiler. The laundry was done by hand, by rubbing the clothes on a washboard in a galvanized tin tub. When ironing, she heated the old-fashioned irons on top of the wood stove. A clothes line, stretched on posts between the bowstable and the boat's stern cabin, served to dry the clothes. The water to bathe the children had to be heated on the stove. The water for drinking and cooking was dippered into a pail from the barrel on deck and carried into the cabin. The sleeping accommodations were increased by adding two more double bunks to those already built into the stateroom, so that it slept eight people instead of four.

There were no built-in bathroom facilities on a canal boat in those days. You washed your hands and face in a tin wash basin or a bucket of water dipped up from the canal. For the women and small children, the toilet was a slop jar containing a small amount of water, kept out of sight in the stateroom. The men and older boys used the bowstable for privacy. A tin bucket was kept there for this purpose, though some preferred to use a shovel and the soiled bedding from the bowstable floor. All waste was disposed of by heaving it overboard. No one was shocked by this practice. There was no alternative, and heaving overboard was the answer to all disposal problems from the time the canal had opened. There was enough clean water coming in from the feeders and runoff from the fields to cause enough current in the canal to take care of this biodegradable material. Some canallers fashioned a wooden toilet seat which fitted on top of the open bucket for more comfort; others just sat on the rim. There was a joke amongst canal boatmen that a drowned canaller could always be identified by the imprint of a ring around his rump from sitting on a bucket. An often repeated family story, connected with this same subject, concerns a cousin of mine who was availing himself of the meager facilities of the bowstable when he was soundly kicked by a mule. He carried a scar in the shape of a mule's shoe on his buttock for the rest of his days.

Raising a family in the small space of a canal boat cabin always kept Mother busy keeping all of us children in line and watching constantly that no one fell overboard. Sometimes to get a toddler out from underfoot and into the fresh air, she would tie the child on top of the cabin with a short piece of clothesline, so that it could move about but could not fall off the cabin or into the canal. This could only be done when the boats were loaded. Nothing could be on the cabin when the boats were light or empty because of the low bridges. If the boats were traveling light, the small children could be put in the empty cargo hold or midship to play. Here they stayed until Mother was ready to have them back in the cabin. She coped with childhood sicknesses, minor injuries, and took small or large emergencies in stride. From the time Mother first went on the canal in 1905 until she made the last trip in 1913, she had gone through some harrowing experiences because of the children. One of the first of them happened to me, and it is also one of my earliest recollections of life on the canal, one that I remember very well although I was very young at the time. The incident happened in 1908, when I was five years old. After unloading at Albany we were on our way up the Champlain Canal toward Lake Champlain to pick up a cargo to carry west. The boats were light, being towed by our mules. My father was steering from the head boat and I was on the stern deck of the after boat, when I decided to go to the bowstable for some reason or other. Father must have been keeping his eye on me because at that age I could not swim and did not have sense enough to be afraid. I grasped the edge of the bowstable hatch and lifted my feet clear of the deck to swing my feet inside when my hands lost their grip and I took a back dive into the canal. I sank clear to the bottom and I was spluttering and paddling my way up when the blurred figure of my father loomed up beside me and took me under his arm and swam to the surface. We crawled up the sloped canal bank and got on the towpath, trotted ahead of the boats and dropped aboard at the next bridge nearby. My father had called to Mother to grab the steering wheel as he ran aft and dove in after me. The boats never stopped during this excitement. After we dropped aboard from the bridge I probably got a good scolding, but if so, I cannot recall it now.

CHAPTER 2

Canal Drivers and Mules

ILLUSTRATIONS of early canal tows pulled by one or two mules or horses show the driver riding on the back of one of the animals. The boats were smaller then and towed easily, especially the packet boats which made close to four miles an hour. When the enlargement of the canal was completed in 1862, the carrying capacity of the boats was more than doubled. The drivers then were no longer allowed to ride the hardworking animals, but, like most rules, this one was not always followed.

The graveyard shift was lonesome and monotonous when there were no locks, towns, or cities to pass through to interrupt the steady plodding along the towpath. Some drivers told of becoming sleepy and taking cat-naps as they walked behind the team with the reins in one hand and the other hand resting on or holding the towline. A few drivers, unable to stay awake, would climb on a mule's back and sleep riding along the towpath.

The driver and team were about two hundred and fifty feet ahead of the boats on a long towline. On dark moonless nights, a steersman could not always see them, but knew they were up ahead pulling the boats along. Should he suspect or become aware of the driver riding one of the animals, with a few choice cuss words he would shout at the culprit to get down. The driver would then be in for a bawling out at changing time. A sleepy driver did not get away with riding one of the animals for very long.

The first time I heard the expression "graveyard shift," it was

17

from canal men. There were places along the canal where ceme-
teries bordered on the towpath. Many of the drivers were very
young; some of the older ones were uneducated and superstitious.
When passing a graveyard, a few of the drivers would tie the reins
to the towline and drop back alongside of the boats and talk to
the steersman, while passing what to them was a spooky place.
There were two stretches along the canal called "haunted levels."
Most drivers preferred to pass by these areas in the daytime.

One of my friends who drove mules for his father at the age
of 12 told me of an experience he once had on the towpath. He
recalled that it was about 11 P.M. on a very dark night, and, as he
neared a bridge crossing over the towpath and canal, the mules
stopped dead in their tracks and could not be made to go on. The
boats drifted down to the team and his father asked what was
wrong. On being told, he grabbed a pikepole, stuck it in the bottom of the canal and vaulted ashore from the drifting boats. Walking ahead of the team, he discovered that a man had committed
suicide by hanging himself from the underside of the bridge over
the towpath. The body had to be cut down and removed before
the mules would go on. This incident did nothing to enhance the
young lad's liking for night driving on the towpath. He also mentioned that he whistled and sang loudly for the mules' benefit
when driving past any graveyards after dark. He tried to convince
his father that he should be riding the boats at night instead of
walking the towpath, but to no avail.

Shortly after this incident my friend's uncle decided to have
some fun with the young driver. The uncle hopped off the boats
one night as they passed under a bridge, and then circled around in
a field beside the towpath. As soon as the team passed by, he
covered himself with a bed sheet and attracted the young boy's
attention by moaning and slowly waving his arms. This second
spooky event almost unnerved the boy. Only his uncle thought
it was funny. The boy continued to drive mules for a few more
seasons until his father gave up the canal boats. In later years my
friend had no fond memories of the towpath, but was rather
bitter that he had been made to do a man's work while still a boy.

My Uncle Charles Kohler, when sixteen, drove mules for my
father for a few seasons on the canal. We were still boating lumber
at the time. He told me of some incidents he remembered while

A boatman about to vault ashore from a moving canal boat. Drawing by E. Mayes.

driving along the towpath. He mentioned the two "haunted levels" on the Erie Canal, and he also recalled the graveyards that were near the towpath. My father knew that driving past these places late at night or in the small hours of the morning was bound to make any young driver uneasy, as well as some of the older ones. One of the experiences that Uncle Charles had took place on the haunted level near Montezuma. The other haunted level was east of Syracuse. He was driving the 1 to 7 A.M. trick and would pass the supposedly haunted house near Montezuma about two o'clock in the morning. Being rather young, he said my father had asked him before going on the towpath at changing time if he had any qualms about driving past the old house at that time of night. He replied that spooks or haunts did not worry him and that he would be all right.

The old house was very near the towpath and got its reputation for being haunted because a murder had been committed there years before. Two brothers had lived in the old house for years. For some reason they had a falling out, and one brother, in a fit of rage, killed the other with an axe as he lay asleep in bed. No one ever lived there after the murder, and it became known as a haunted house. With its windows all broken, door hanging awry, and most of the roofing blown away, it was an eerie place to pass in the darkness. Although he admitted to being a bit nervous as the team approached the old house, he did not expect any trouble. All went well until the mules were directly opposite the house, when suddenly they stopped dead in their tracks and, in spite of his commands, they refused to move on. He suddenly panicked and could not decide if he should jump in the canal and swim over to the boats, or run back along the towpath, away from the old house. When he calmed down a bit he could see nothing wrong and finally got up his courage and walked past the stopped mules. A short way ahead of the team, he found a strip of tarpaper stretched across the towpath that had blown from the roof of the old house. With a huge sigh of relief he removed the roofing from the towpath. The mules then continued on with the tow. The team had simply refused to step on or across the roofing paper.

There were also canal drivers who were mature men. Some came from farms; others had driven teams before hiring out on the canal. They were used to animals and knew how to manage them.

This was their only responsibility, and they sought no other. In some cases when the boat owner or operator had a boy old enough to drive a team, he would be pressed into service as a driver. The boy had to be clothed and fed anyway, and it saved the board and wages of a man.

While passing through the canal, drivers worked twelve hours each day, six hours on and six hours off. Changing teams and meal times were at 7:00 A.M., 1:00 P.M., 7:00 P.M., and 1:00 A.M., at which time a midnight lunch was set out for each member of the crew in the after cabin. This was the standard schedule on canal fleets. I believe it was kept so that the cook did not have to rise too early.

The driver was awakened one hour before changing time to water, feed, and harness the team. While the animals were feeding, the driver washed up; then he and one steersman went back to the after cabin and ate together. As soon as they came back on deck, the steersman on duty called to the driver on the towpath to look for a tie-up post. At times a tree or telegraph pole was used for this purpose. As soon as the boats were stopped, the mules were unhitched from the towline and the horse or change bridge was run out from the boats to the canal bank.

The fresh mules were run ashore, then the tired mules were guided aboard the boat, and the horsebridge was pulled aboard. By that time the fresh team had been hitched to the towline. The tie-up lines were let go and the boats were under way again within fifteen minutes or so. Everything went like clockwork at changing time. The steersman and the driver who had just been relieved washed up, then went back to the after cabin and ate. When the meal was finished, the driver returned to the bowstable, where he watered and fed the team and then removed their harnesses while they were eating. He then cleaned the stable floor, by sweeping the manure and soiled bedding material into a pile and, with the help of a scoop shovel, threw it from the stable into the canal. He then spread about one inch of bedding material over the floor (shavings or sawdust) to help soak up any animal urine. When he had finished taking care of the team he rested until it was time to get them ready for the next six-hour shift or trick on the towpath.

Uncle Charles also told of changing teams without completely stopping the boats, if there were no tie-up posts or trees along the canal at changing time. The team would stop towing, and, as the boats lost headway, they would be steered in close to the towpath, slowly drifting along with the current. The end of the horse bridge would be put ashore. The other driver or steersman would then run ashore and help move the horse bridge along the towpath by the attached pull lines. It had to be kept abreast of the bowstable door after each animal had been run ashore or aboard the boat. This could only be done during the daylight hours, or on a bright moonlit night. It was risky to attempt in the darkness or in a strong current.

Another incident that happened on one trip concerned an old and clumsy mule. While coming ashore at changing time, the mule stumbled on the horse bridge and fell into the canal. He went completely under the water and did not come up right away. The crew said, "To heck with him. We won't be bothered by that knothead anymore." Suddenly the animal came to the surface, climbed up the sloping canal bank, walked along the towpath, took his own place in the team, and stood there waiting to be hitched up to the towline. After a few seasons on the canal mules would get on and off the boat at changing time by themselves. They knew their place in the bowstable and on the towpath.

I have been asked many times why mules were used on the canal instead of horses. I knew that canal men considered the mules smarter in many ways. They were also more nimble and surer-footed, climbing in and out of bowstables and up and down horse bridges, were less skittish, and not so apt to be alarmed over unusual sights or sounds along the towpath. Canal animals drank from a bucket of water dipped up from the canal. A horse might drink water contaminated by sewage and become sick, but a mule would refuse it no matter how thirsty it might be.

Another factor was that the hindmost part of a horse sways when it walks or climbs. This sometimes caused it to stumble or miss its footing while getting on or off canal boats.

One encyclopedia describes the mule as a hybrid offspring of a male jackass and a mare (female horse), saying that the "head, ears, and croup and tail show prepotency of the ass, but in bulk and stature the mule is nearer the horse and seems to excel both its parents in sagacity, muscular endurance, sure-footedness and length of life." I remember reading an account credited to the old

Niles Register that recorded the remarkable feat of a female mule giving birth to a colt. But this "unique case" was doubted by most people, because mules were incapable of propagating or even producing a cross-breed.

The animals' cabin or stable was always on the front end or bow of any canal boat, and it was called the bow (bough) stable. It was twelve feet wide by about nine feet long. In a lumber boat bowstable the mules always faced forward, toward the front end of the boat. Sliding wooden doors or shutters over the feed boxes or mangers were most always kept open for ventilation. There were no shutters or openings on the back of the stable because, when the boats were loaded, lumber was piled against the rear end of the stable. Baled hay and oats were the staple feed for canal animals; and they were occasionally given a measure of corn as well to vary their diet.

The hay and bedding materials such as shavings or sawdust were stored under the bow deck, forward to the mangers or feed boxes. Oats, corn, collars, and harness parts were stored in cupboards under the side decks on each side of the bowstable. The animals were watered from a bucket dipped up from the canal.

When the time came to change teams, if the animals were veterans, everything went smoothly. The three mules aboard the boat were faced toward the towpath side of the stable, and the inside cleated bridges were hooked into place. This center mule was then under the bowstable hatch opening, and it was the first one out. The other two followed in proper order, the animals when leaving the stable actually scrambling up the steep inside bridges. When coming aboard, the center mule was the last one to enter the stable. The inside bridges were removed, and the three mules were turned at the same time to face the front of the boat.

The bowstable floor was about three and a half feet below the deck of a canal boat. This made the inside bridges very steep. The animals usually left the stable without help. When entering the stable, the steersman or driver grasped the tail and held back on the animal so that it did not stumble or enter too fast. A short line was fastened to each corner of the horse bridge and when it was shoved out part way, the lines were tossed to the driver on the towpath, who assisted in getting the end of it ashore. The horse bridge was made of oak; it was kept as light as possible but had to

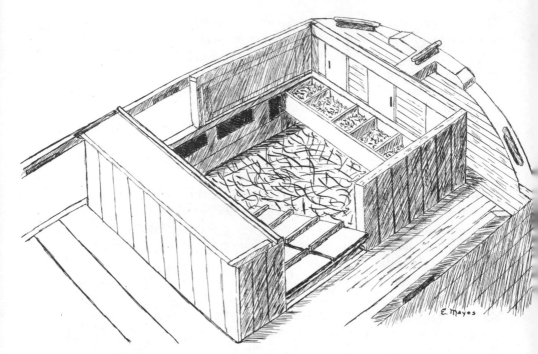

An open view of a lumber boat bowstable; the feedboxes or mangers are shown at the forward end of the stable. The cleated inside bridges or ramps are hooked in place, ready for the mules to enter. Drawing by E. Mayes.

be strong enough to support the weight of a mule or horse. It was stowed on top of the bowstable on a loaded lumber boat, but when the boat was light, it had to be stowed in back of the stable, on what was called a "dead hatch" or platform over the midship, else it could be damaged or swept away by low bridges.

Bowstable floors were below deck level on a canal boat, and cargo was stowed in the four-and-one-half-foot space between the floor and the bottom of the cargo hold, in both the lumber and grain boats. The floors of sturdy construction were double floored of the best grade of lumber. The subfloor was of the same material as the side of the boat and of clear white pine, four to five inches thick by eight inches wide. They were built to last the life of the boat. The seams in the bottom floor were pitched and caulked to prevent any animal seepage from contaminating the cargo. In addition, a heavy coat of roofing tar was spread over the entire floor.

A top floor of two-inch hardwood was then nailed down over the fresh tar. This floor was replaced when it started to wear through because of the scuffing from the mules' iron shoes.

The end of animal power on the canal was welcomed by most of the canal men, because they knew the animals were overworked. It was hard and tedious for a team pulling for six long hours on the towpath.

The action of a mule's forelegs caused the collar to move slightly on the animal's breast as he pulled steadily on the towline. The collar movement chafed some of the hide off of the mule's breast under the collar, causing large sores or raw spots. The canallers called them "gall marks." Different types of salve and other medications were kept on hand to treat the sore spots. These only helped to ease the soreness because the gall marks would heal up only when the animals were put out to pasture and given a few weeks' rest. Even then, a few days back on the towpath pulling steadily would cause the sore spots to reappear. Although the gall marks were ugly to look at and sensitive when touched or treated, they did not seem to affect the animal's pulling power or his willingness to work.

During the last few years of animal power on the Erie Canal, when the boats passed through large cities, the local SPCA agents stopped the mules and examined their breasts. If the animals were badly galled they were taken off the towpath and pastured out until their breasts were healed. In some cases a fine was imposed on the owner of the team. No doubt this punitive action would have soon ended the use of mules or horses on the canal, in favor of mechanical power. It caused delays to canal men, and any animal removed from a team also meant overworking the other animals.

The towpath was a mixture of clay and gravel, hard packed from the hoofs of the plodding mules. The surface was usually sprinkled with small stones, which did not bother the steel-shod mules, but some drivers complained of sore feet. The sore feet were caused more by personal neglect than anything else because the canallers resisted taking a bath and changing their clothes, when they should have done so. This may have been because they had to wash their own clothes. In the summer a bath was had by soaping up and taking a dip in the canal. When the weather was cool, it was just too much bother. Those who became itchy would rather scratch than take a bath and change clothes. They also claimed that scratching kept them warm as they walked along the towpath on cool evenings.

Canal drivers were mostly happy-go-lucky, with little or no family ties. They had to be on the towpath in all kinds of weather, night and day, rain or shine. Their wages in the early 1900s were one dollar a day and board. Most of the drivers were hired by the trip and were paid off at either end of the canal. There was no work for them while the boats were loading or unloading, which might take from three days to a week or more. Sometimes they would stay aboard the boats and look after the animals for their meals and a place to sleep. Usually they went on a spree until their money was spent and then hired out again to the first boat owner who required their services for the next trip, east or west.

Working and living the kind of life that was typical of canal mule drivers at that time, they seldom had any money at the end of the canal season. Some of them sought work driving teams in the large cities, while others went back to their homes, if they had them. It was habitual with some of these men to commit some minor offense against the law, or contrive to get arrested for vagrancy. Spending the winter in a nice warm jail, they hoped to be let out when the canal opened in the spring. Some of the canal men saved their money during the summer and then made a deal with a hotel or boarding house keeper to board them for the winter for a lump sum. One hundred dollars or less would board a man for the winter in those days. While the canal man might run out of money before the winter was over, he still had a room and a place to eat until navigation opened in the spring.

The nicknames of some of the mule drivers identified the locality from which they came. To name a few who were well known on the canal, there was "Oswego Dutch," "Rhode Island Red," and "Bohemian Dutch." Other nicknames were descriptive of the person or his characteristics, such as "Squirrel" Wheeler, "Shivery" Newman, "Monkey" Joe, and Sam "Dime," who was always asking if any one had two nickels for an old dime.

Some of these men were casual acquaintances of ours. Shivery Newman and some of the others had driven mules for my father. Shivery got his nickname from having the shakes after he had been drinking, which was at the end of each trip. Monkey Joe was a short, bowlegged, wiry man, a native of Tonawanda, who spent most of his life on the canal. Sam Dime drove mules for my father for a good many seasons on the canal and he had sort of adopted our family as his own. He was quite old by the time my father had disposed of his mules. A few seasons after this took place he showed up at our house and asked my father to get him placed in the Erie County Home, which was done a short time later.

Driving a team along the towpath in the daytime when the weather was good had its pleasant side, but in the rain and snow it was miserable.

Many of the drivers liked and followed this work for years, and some stayed at it all their lives. These men liked animals and the chance to be out in the open, and they enjoyed going through the countryside at a leisurely pace behind the mules. There were many things to see while passing through the large cities, towns, and villages and the scenic and peaceful countryside. There were many old acquaintances to greet when meeting or passing other canal tows. Going through the locks gave the driver and team a twenty minute or half-hour rest. Here the driver watered the mules, stepped aboard the boats, or got a drink of water and a sandwich, if he was hungry. He also put out the stern line in the lock so that the other steersman did not have to get out of bed when locking through.

The mules were thoroughly trained after a few months on the towpath and pulled steadily on straight stretches along the canal without anyone guiding them. Occasionally the driver tied the reins to the towline when passing by a canalside orchard and stepped in and helped himself to whatever fruit might be in season.

The same thing often happened at corn and tomato fields. The driver filled his hat with whatever produce was available, got alongside and tossed it one by one to the steersman on the moving boats. If the farm house happened to be out of sight of the canal, a stray chicken or duck strolling along or near the towpath found its way into the canaller's stew pot in the same manner.

Many an irate farmer kept these depredations under control by firing a charge of rocksalt over the heads of the offenders. News of this nature travelled the length of the canal quickly, and the property of the shotgun owner was treated with due respect thereafter.

Although the average driver was somewhat of a rascal, all those employed by my father were respectful to Mother and they liked children. The driver's soothing voice and firm hands on the reins kept the team pulling steadily through heavy rain, thunder and lightning storms. He calmed the mules frightened by dogs snapping at their heels or snakes slithering across the towpath.

Canal drivers seldom if ever talked of their home towns or their family backgrounds. They never seemed to plan for the future and were content with a day-to-day existence. Their greatest failing and weakness was over-indulgence in whiskey. They were frequently broke and hungry and often begged drinks and food from canal men they knew until they hired out again. None of these drawbacks influenced very many of them to change their way of life. They were a footloose breed of men, all gone now along with the old towpath.

CHAPTER 3

Steersmen, Bank Watchers, and Cooks

T HE CANAL BOAT STEERSMEN that I knew were usually respon- sible and steady men. Many of them started on the canal as young men and never married. Beginning as drivers, they had thoroughly learned the business and had advanced to the position of second in command. Theirs was a responsible job and many of them were on hand at the beginning of each season to work for the same boat owners.

In the early 1900s a steersman's wages were sixty dollars a month and board. Sometimes a few of them went on a spree dur- ing the season. As a rule they were sober when the boats were ready to start over the canal. A steersman slept on the head boat and was in charge of its loading or unloading. Working six hours on and six hours off, he most always had the 1 to 7 trick, night and day, in all kinds of weather. Like the driver on the towpath, he had no protection from the elements, except for a set of oilskin rain gear. Meeting and passing other tows safely, he steered and guided the boats around crooked bends, across aqueducts, and in and out of locks, where he handled lines while passing through.

The steersman had to be on hand at changing time to help tie up the boats. He also helped to put the horse bridge ashore and assisted in getting the mules on and off the boats. His rest was sometimes broken up when passing through locks or when troubles arose along the canal. He was expected to make himself generally useful at all times. It was traditional on the canal for the boat owner or senior steersman and driver to work the 7 to 1 trick. Working these hours was a more normal way of life. It was more natural to have a nap in the afternoon, then work the first part of the evening and have a good sleep from 1 to 7 A.M. The man coming off the late shift went to bed soon after breakfast; he then worked the afternoon trick and must lay down early in the evening to rest for the late-night trick, on which it was an ordeal for some to stay awake until changing time.

There were places along the Erie Canal where the towpath changed from one side to the other. This was because of engineering difficulties and changes in the terrain. The mules and driver crossed the canal on bridges especially designed for this purpose. They were called "change bridges" or "towpath bridges." When the mules approached the bridge, they kept pulling as they walked up the ramp, which sloped up to the bridge. When the towline went slack, the driver grasped it and held back on the whiffletrees so they did not bang against the heels of the team as they walked across the wooden-plank bridge. While the line was slack the steersman changed it to the proper side of the head boat's bow. After crossing the bridge, the team turned and went down a ramp leading to the towpath on the other side of the canal. The driver would hold back on the whiffletrees until the slack was taken out of the towline. The bridge and its approaches were so arranged that the crossing was made without letting go of the towline. While the team was crossing the bridge the boats kept drifting onward. Very little time was lost changing towpaths.

The towpath was on the north side of the canal from Albany to Camillus, a village on the Erie seven miles west of Syracuse. From Camillus westward there were twelve towpath change bridges along the canal. The last one was at Jersey Street in Buffalo.

Thinking of towpaths brings recollections of the lone men I used to see walking along the canal banks. They were called "bank watchmen" or inspectors. At many places along the Erie, the canal banks were higher than the countryside through which it passed. The watchman's duty was to check for any leaks that might grow larger and cause breaks or washouts in the canal banks. He usually carried a shovel to repair small leaks and reported any large leaks to the Division Boss, who would rush a repair crew to the scene.

A team and canal boats approaching the towpath change bridge at the foot of Gibson Street in Tonawanda, N.Y. Also in view are lumber piles along the Niagara River and a steamer on the right bound for the lumber docks. Drawing by E. Mayes.

Muskrats and other small animals were the frequent causes of leaks or washouts. In the early days of the canal, competitors such as freight-hauling teamsters and stage coach lines, whose business was affected by the opening of the canal, deliberately dug holes in the canal banks which drained the canal and tied up navigation. These people did not believe competition was the life of trade, for they tried to eliminate it entirely.

A cook was an essential part of a canal boat crew, but by the early 1900s very few cooks were left on the Erie Canal. As most boatmen had their wives and families with them on the boats, there was no problem about the cook. If the captain was single or a widower, he tried to hire a married steersman so that the wife could cook for the entire crew. These couples were usually hired at a joint wage and given the after boat cabin for living quarters.

It was a hardship for any boatman to operate a pair of boats without a cook. In a four-man crew, each worked six hours on and six hours off. Without a cook, it was usually the captain who got up ahead of time and prepared the meal. The steersman or the off-duty driver washed the dishes and cleaned up the cabin. With this arrangement, the cooking left something to be desired and the cabin got too much of a lived-in look, with no one getting enough rest.

On arriving at Tonawanda, if a boatman inquired for a cook, he might be told to look up "Old Black Nell." Nell was not Negro, but she was very dark complexioned. She could usually be found keeping house for some of the painted ladies on Goose Island. Old she might have been, but Nell was still not beyond bestowing her favors on any gentleman who happened to seek her out while housekeeping. If the boatman was desperate, she was hired. I believe Nell was a good enough cook, and being of a generous nature, well past the age of innocence, she did not care who shared the cabin with her. As a rule, she lasted for only one round trip, for on returning to Tonawanda, she would draw some of her wages and go ashore to visit. On returning from her "visit," she would be drunk as Satan and, supplied with a bottle of whiskey, she would not bother about getting any meals. A big argument would then ensue, and she would get fired. Nell was a quite peppery and noisy old dame when full of whiskey.

I once saw "Old Black Nell" passing George Huber's store on North Niagara Street after she had been fired from one of her cook's jobs. She was hanging on to her hat, which was cocked to one side of her head, her long black sateen skirt dragging on the sidewalk, and her suitcase partly shut with some of her clothing dangling from it. She was looking back, mumbling and cursing about the unappreciative qualities of the boatman who had fired her.

I don't know which disappeared from the local scene first, the Erie Canal boats or "Old Black Nell."

A captain who had his family on the boats lived a fairly comfortable life, as the woman had the meals on time, did the washing and ironing, kept the cabin clean, and made the beds. She also saw that her husband had a bath occasionally so that he did not get lousy as many other bathless canallers did.

During the canning season many canalmen's wives purchased fruit and vegetables at locks or canalside stores or from farmers along the canal. The boater's wife canned and preserved things in the cabin of the boat, and when the boat was laid up in the fall, the canned goods were taken home for winter use. On the final trip in the fall many families purchased two or three barrels of different kinds of apples, ten or twenty bushels of potatoes, a supply of cabbage and quantities of beets, turnips, squash, and other vegetables. These they stored in their earthen-floored cellars and used during the winter.

The first day after starting up or down the canal, fresh meat was usually on the menu. After that, the ice was gone. Then, smoked and salted meats were the general fare until the boats stopped at a canalside grocery store, where the ice and the depleted larder were again replenished. There were many such stores at intervals along the canal. A few of the locks had adjoining grocery stores, and supplies could be bought while locking through.

Canalside stores stocked anything a canal fleet needed in the way of patent medicines, cooking pots, tinware, candy, food, shoes, clothing, rain gear, and dry goods. Also available were supplies such as hay, oats, straw or shavings, harnesses, horse collars, whiffletrees, towlines, horsebridges, fenders, pike poles, and hardware. It was also possible to take on drinking and cooking water at these places. Kerosene or coal oil had to be obtained at these supply points, as oil lamps were the only type of illumination to be had on canal boats at that time.

On a pair of canal boats, the family living quarters were usually on the stern or second boat, which some canallers called "the family boat." Here the crew as well as the family were fed in the stern boat's cabin. This arrangement gave the family more privacy when passing through the canal, as the steersman was always near the cabin of the head boat. It was also more quiet for sleeping as there was always noise and commotion on the head boat when passing through locks or changing teams.

When the boats were separated, a basket of food was prepared for the steersman, who stayed on the head boat; if it was used up, he ate ashore until the boats were again joined together. The only time the boats became separated was when they were loaded or unloaded at different towns or docks.

Home-made bread, pies, cookies, roasts, etc., were baked in the oven of the black iron cook stove in the cabin. Fuel for cooking or heating was never a problem on lumber boats because the boatman sawed up what lumber was needed for firewood from the cargo.

CHAPTER 4

Lock Operations

Lockport had the only double or twinned locks on the original Erie Canal. At all other places on the canal upbound and downbound traffic used the same lock. All distances between locks were called "levels"—sixty-mile level, nine-mile level, etc. These were level stretches of canal between locks, each one a different height above sea level. The canal rose 564.8 feet from Albany to Buffalo. The first boats carried 40 tons and did not completely fill a lock. As time went by, the size of the boats was increased; they carried 75 tons and filled the lock to its entire capacity. After the canal enlargement was completed in 1862, its length was shortened 12½ miles or from 363 to 350½ miles. The freight-carrying capacity of the boats and the canal was more than doubled. The number of locks on the canal was reduced from 83 to 72. The size of the locks was increased and had seven feet of water (instead of four) over the mitre sills. The mitre sills were two pieces of timber about eight inches square, which formed a sort of triangle and were bolted to the bottom of the lock. The sills were a stop for the lock gates and reinforced them when the gates were closed and the lock filled with water. The height of the bridges was increased to eleven feet above the canal, still scant clearance when the boats were light or empty. When the enlargement had been completed all of the seventy-two locks had been twinned; but were still single in length; one could be used for up-bound and the other for downbound traffic. They were called the heelpath and the towpath locks. In 1884 lengthening of one of the twin locks was begun in order to accommodate two-boat tows or a double header. Canal men always referred to tows passing through the canal as a single header, double header, triple header, or quadruple header. The animal-towed boats seldom exceeded a triple header. Quadruple headers were usually towed by steam canal boats after 1884, when all of the single locks had been lengthened. The lengthening of one lock saved considerable time. A single header used the single lock, a double header locked through without uncoupling the boats. With a triple header, the third or last boat was uncoupled and cut loose from the two head boats a short way above the locks. It had sufficient headway to be steered by its own rudder over into the single lock. This permitted the three boats to be locked through at the same time. Quadruple headers locked two at a time through the double or lengthened lock. If the lock was filled and the gates opened when the boats arrived, a double header could be locked through and on its way in fifteen minutes or less. Delays were frequent at locks if other boats were locking up or down at the same time we arrived. The five twinned locks (flights) at Lockport were always single locks. One set of them is still there. They had a stone-arch foot bridge below each set of lower gates. When the boats were lowered in the lock they passed beneath the foot bridge into the next lock. Most of the locks beyond Lockport had wooden foot bridges just ahead or below the lower gates. Foot bridges ahead of the lower gates were elevated and had a flight of stairs on each side of the lock, which one had to climb to cross over the lock when the lower set of gates were open. The purpose of the foot bridge was to save the locktender time and footsteps when boats were passing through the locks. The foot bridge was always at the lower end of the lock. After upbound boats were in the lock, the locktender closed one gate. Without a foot bridge on the lengthened or double locks, he would have had to walk 220 feet to the closed upper gates to cross over the lock, then back again to the lower end of the lock to close the other gate.

The Erie Canal lock at Buffalo between Austin and Hamilton Streets was a guard lock. Here the boats passed directly through, unless the Lake Erie water level was too much above normal. This sometimes occurred during prolonged westerly windstorms. There

Erie and Cayuga-Seneca Canal junction lock on the west side of the village of Montezuma, N.Y., and the locktender's shanty in the background. The lock-tender is holding a paddle valve lever while a friend stands nearby.

was another guard lock two miles east of Pendleton, which was usually closed at the end of the navigation season, permitting the canal to be emptied between the guard lock and Rochester. Maintenance work could then be done at the Lockport locks and on this section of the canal during the winter. This lock protected Lockport and the long level from the flood waters of Tonawanda Creek during the spring runoff of melted snow and rain. It was also a safeguard, should a mechanical failure occur at the locks, such as a boat crashing through the gates when entering the lock. This twin guard lock had a center pier in the middle of the canal. The approach walls at each end of the lock were very short, and it was a hazardous place to pass through, even though the tows were slowed somewhat. A steersman had to have the boats lined up perfectly or they would strike the center pier and be damaged or sunk. This type of accident happened a number of times at this particular lock.

Most of the old Erie Canal locks had two swinging wooden gates at each end of the lock, which closed against a mitre sill at the bottom of the lock. The gate edges were also mitered to resist the pressure of the water when the lock was full. Each gate had two valves in it to empty or fill the lock. The valves were just flat boards about twelve by twenty-four inches, pivoted in the middle and hand-operated by a four-foot lever attached by bell cranks and linkage to the valves in the gates. After the boats were lowered in the lock the lower gates were opened, and one or two of the valves or paddles in the closed upper gates were opened. The water rushing through the valves flushed or swelled the boats out of the lock because the sudden rush of water could not get around the boat. The early lock builders designated this type of valve built into the gate, a paddle valve. Locktenders and canal men called the valves "paddles." Each gate on the lock had a long wooden balance beam attached to it to balance the gate, which hung on a sort of hinge. The balance beam made it possible to operate the gate manually. Many times as a boy, I put my back against the gate's balance beam and pushed with the locktender to open or close the gate. I was never allowed to touch the paddles because of the danger of being injured when the lock was being filled or emptied. When the paddle valves were being operated, the water on reaching a certain position pushed against the paddle valve with a force strong enough to tear the paddle lever out of one's hands. No harm was done if this happened when one stood on the proper side. If the operator stood on the wrong side of the lever, however, it could knock him into the canal. There were quite a number of injuries and drownings due to the improper operation of lock paddles. This type of valve built into the gate had to be operated from a foot plank about twelve inches wide that was attached to each gate. The paddles were usually operated with one hand, while the other hand gripped the railing that was fastened to each gate. This type of gate and the valves for filling and emptying was the most common in use on the Erie Canal locks in my canal days. At the upper end of a few of the locks, a tumble gate replaced the usual swing-type gates. When a boat entered or left the lock the tumble gate was released and fell by gravity to the bottom. The boats entering or leaving the lock, passed over the gate which was raised or closed by a chain attached to each corner. It was powered by a hand-cranked windlass on each side of the lock. The valves that filled the lock were located ahead of the gate at each side of the lock and were tunneled around the gate. The valves were also operated by a chain and hand-cranked windlass, with the water entering from the side of the lock. This arrangement was not as efficient as the paddle-type valve for swelling a boat out of a lock.

"Swelling" was a term familiar to all canal men. The swells were caused by the sudden opening of the paddle valves in the lock gates. Swells were also caused by emptying the lock when boats were locking down or by emptying the lock to get it ready for an approaching tow. It was often necessary to swell loaded lumber boats from the locks after they had been lowered down as they always had some list to them because of the high deckload, which made them slightly topheavy. If the list became too great it was partly righted by carrying a few boards from one side of the boat to the other. If one tried to get the boat perfectly level it would list in the other direction; they were never level when fully loaded. Entering a lock with a list often caused a lumber boat to bind in the lock after it was lowered. Ordinarily as soon as the lower gates were opened the towline from the team was made fast to the head boat. The mules then pulled the boats from the lock and were on their way. However, if the boats were hard to start or would not start at all, the locktender would open a paddle or two and start the boats moving. A slight swell always got the boats started faster, and shortened the time locking through. If the locktender happened to be a good fellow, he gave the boats a swell without being asked. Some of them would not give the boats a swell unless they were first given the price of a couple of beers, which in those days cost a nickel. For a dime you could really be speeded on your way. If the boats were hung up hard in the lock, some of the locktenders would hold out for a quarter. A loud argument might take place, but it was pay or be stuck. The practice of swelling was frowned on by canal authorities. It used too much canal water and lowered the water on the level above the lock, which at times caused loaded boats to run aground. Swelling also raised the water on the level below the lock, causing the

Canal boat being swelled out of lower downbound lock at Lockport, N.Y.
Photo *circa* 1890s.

cabins on light or empty boats to strike the low bridges, thus causing extensive damage. I recall loaded boats running aground when
they met or passed other loaded tows; if the team could not pull
them off, they would wait for a swell from the locks to get them
moving. At times they were stuck so hard that word was sent back
to the last lock requesting an extra heavy swell. This was done by
opening all the paddle valves on the lock gates at the same time.
This created a swell or surge that traveled the whole length of the
shorter levels. The swells were not very noticeable on the longer
levels unless you were near a lock. There were times when a swell
was not sufficient or available to free a pair of grounded boats.
A good strong line would be made ready. Then when the next
loaded tow came by the men on the tow were requested to fasten
the line to a cleat on the stern of the moving boats, which they

usually did. A man on the head end of the grounded boats then took a few turns around a cleat with the line, and began snubbing. He used the weight and the headway of the moving tow to free the grounded boats.

"Snubbing" was a term and a method much in use when animal power was on the canal. The animals could not be reversed to stop the boats as they do today with the engines. To stop moving boats at a certain place, a line was made ready and fastened to a post or cleat on the dock or shore. A few turns were then taken around a cleat or pair of bitts on the boat. The boats were stopped by rendering the line around the cleat or bitts, while maintaining sufficient tension to bring the boats to a stop. When entering locks on the Erie Canal, a line kept dry and in good condition, two and a half inches in diameter by sixty feet long, was made fast to a side cleat on the bow of the head boat. The locks had snubbing posts, about 25 feet apart, along the length of the lock. When the moving boats had entered the lock, the boatman stepped ashore with the line and began snubbing the headway from the boats, moving from post to post as he did so. This was a meticulous job; the boats must be brought to a stop before they hit the lower gates, yet be in the lock far enough to close the upper gates.

CHAPTER 5

Lumber and Grain Boats

IN THE early canal days there were numerous boat yards and dry docks all along the canal. In the 1880s there were six boat yards still building grain and lumber boats in the Tonawandas. The last one to operate there was the Ira M. Rose Boat Yard and Drydock. Located on Ellicott Creek, it built the last animal-powered boats in 1905. It then changed hands and continued to build Erie Canal size steam canal fleets until 1912, closing down at the end of that year. The completion of the new and larger Barge Canal was only five years away.

The size of the lumber boats built in Tonawanda were 16 feet wide by 96 feet long, with sides 9 feet high. They were built especially for carrying lumber to the various cities along the canal and to New York City. The draft was 6 feet when loaded and 16 to 18 inches when light. Grain boats were of the same dimensions, except for 10 feet high sides and a more spacious cabin. Carrying 180,000 to 200,000 board feet of lumber or from 210 to 240 tons of bulk cargo such as sand, stone, gravel, steel, and pig iron, the boats were usually coupled together in pairs and towed by a three-span team of mules. There were some triple headers, towed by a four-unit team. The average speed of two loaded boats when towed by three mules was about two miles an hour when going east and two and one half miles an hour, when light or empty, going west. Most of the way east or going down the canal, a slight current aided the progress of the loaded tows; coming west the current had an oppo-

Erie Canal lumber boat under construction at the Ira M. Rose boatyard in Tonawanda, N.Y. Drawing by E. Mayes.

site effect. A light boat drew 16 inches of water, compared to 6 feet when loaded, and therefore towed faster going west, although it was against the current.

Loaded animal-towed boats were seldom loaded deeper than 4 feet, which gave them a capacity of 100 tons when going west, because of the current. Loading them deeper would have slowed their progress too much and overworked the animals. Grain-carrying boats were also built in the Tonawandas. Better built and more costly than lumber boats, they had slightly higher sides, also better and larger living quarters.

Grain, being heavier than lumber, did not completely fill the cargo space. This left room for more spacious cabins. Grain was easily damaged by water. Grain boats had strong watertight decks and watertight hatches that covered the cargo hold. The interior of

A pair of eastbound grain boats leaving Lockport, N.Y. A set of bow lamps are stowed between the bowstable shutters. The sectional wheelhouse must be taken down when the boats pass through the canal empty. Note high stack on passenger train engine on high-level railroad bridge. Photo *circa* early 1900s.

the cargo hold was lined with a good grade of matched lumber to keep the grain from coming in contact with the sides of the boat, and this prevented seepage from damaging the cargo. Grain boats had to be kept in tip-top condition, for if they leaked top, sides, or bottom the grain would be damaged. Although the cargoes were insured against total loss, the first so many bushels damaged were deducted from the boat owner's freight revenue.

Aboard a pair of lumber boats the stern cabin of the second boat was used for living quarters. The inside dimensions were 12 feet wide by 9 or 10 feet long. The cabins were smaller than those on grain boats, because larger cabins cut down the amount of lumber a boat could carry. This was important to the boat owner, as he was paid so much per thousand board feet or fraction thereof.

The cabin was furnished with the barest essentials. If there were small children, it had a rocking chair and a kitchen table, usually covered with oilcloth, and four or five stools that were stored under the table when not in use. The meals were prepared on a black wood- and coal-burning cookstove. The floor was either painted or covered with linoleum, and curtains were hung at the windows. Illumination was provided by a kerosene lamp in a bracket on the wall over the table. There was no fly screening on the windows or on the cabin door and hatch. At mealtime Mother used to shoo the flies out of the cabin with a fly chaser. The part of the cabin used for sleeping quarters extended under the stern deck and was always called the stateroom. This room—about 15 feet wide by 6½ feet long—took up the full inside width of the boat. The floor was about two feet lower than the cabin floor. To enter it, we had to duck our heads to go through a 4-foot-high opening and step down two or three steps. Little or no sunshine ever entered the stateroom; it was always very dim or dark and somewhat damp and musty. The darkness provided some advantage, because when we wished to sleep in the daytime, the flies had a hard time finding the sleeper.

The storage space in the cabin of a lumber boat was very limited. Many of the things used in the cabin were stored on deck. A deck box and an ice chest were kept near the stern boat's cabin. The deck box held potatoes and other vegetables. The ice chest, being metal lined and insulated, held about 150 pounds of ice; here fresh meat, butter, milk, and other perishables were stored. Things stayed fresh longer when kept out of the cabin in the summer. Two drinking water barrels stood near the cabin door. On an empty lumber boat the water barrels and deck boxes were moved to the front of the stern cabin on a platform over the empty cargo hold. Nothing could be carried on the stern deck, because it would interfere with the tiller stick which operated the rudder when the boat was light or empty.

When the boats were loaded with lumber the deck boxes and water barrels were again shifted to the stern deck behind the cabin or on the platform above the cabin, which provided more space for the storage of lumber and also kept deck boxes and the water barrels handy for the cook.

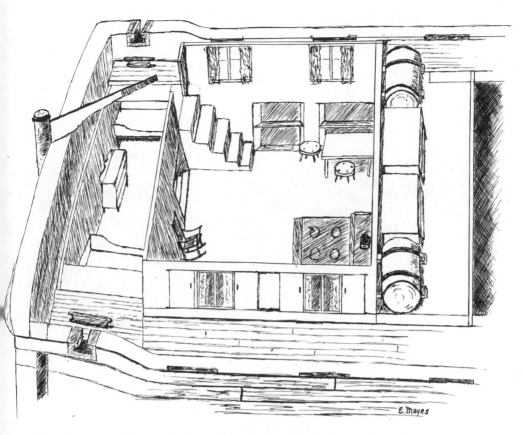

With the roof and stern deck removed the interior of the cabin and the state-room of a lumber boat can be seen. Water barrels, an ice chest, and a vegetable box are shown forward of the cabin. Drawing by E. Mayes.

A lumber boat's cargo was piled about four feet higher than the cabin top and arranged so that an elevated platform built up from the cargo allowed the boatman to see over the deckload and steer the boat with the stern rudder when necessary. To do this an S-shaped tiller or rudder stick was installed in the boat's rudder post instead of the short, straight tiller. Although it was not used too often, the rudder, or blade as it was sometimes called, had to be kept operative at all times. There were certain places along the canal where the boats were guided by this means only.

Lumber boats, after unloading downstate, most always re-

Loaded lumber boats, May 12, 1905, Tonawanda, N.Y., ready to start down the canal, then scheduled to open in a few days. *Buffalo and Erie County Historical Society.*

turned to Tonawanda light or empty. Moving along at the slow speed of two and one half miles per hour, they were subject to being windbound by strong winds. To help avoid this type of delay a canal boat centerboard was developed to help keep the boards in the center of the canal and away from the banks on windy days. It was made of oak planks, driftbolts and strap iron, and sturdy iron posts which helped bind it together. It was 36 inches wide by 25 or 30 feet long and installed in place as soon as the boat was unloaded. It was always removed before the boat was to be loaded.

A leeboard was another contrivance canallers used to fight the wind. Its purpose was to keep the stern of the hind boat from scraping on the stones that lined the sloping canal banks when the wind was blowing toward the towpath. It hung over the side at the stern of the hind boat and had to be pulled on deck when entering a lock, or it could be torn from the side of the boat. The value of a leeboard was doubtful, for it rode up the sloping canal bank when the wind forced the moving boat against the towpath.

It was not unusual for a boat to start leaking while passing through the canal. This could happen when a boat dragged along the bank, or if it had a hard bump when entering a lock. Sharp stones could pull the oakum from the seams, or if it became rotten it was forced through the seams into the boat by water pressure. Whatever the reason for the leak, it meant hours of backbreaking labor at the single-stroke, tin hand pump used on canal boats at that time. The leaks could usually be stopped temporarily by the use of a manure box, and most all canal fleets had at least one. The box was about 16 inches square, fastened to a pole about 12 feet long. Filled with manure and litter from the bowstable floor and with the open side of the box held tightly to the side of the boat, it was shoved under water, just below the bottom of the boat—near the leak, we hoped. The contents of the box floated up to the bottom of the boat and were pulled into the leak by the action of the water. This method of stopping leaks was known as *puddling*. There were times when it took a lot of puddling to find and stop a leak! The manure box was sometimes called a poor man's drydock.

The State of New York maintained wrecking equipment on each of the three divisions on the Erie Canal—Eastern Division (from Albany to Utica), Middle Division (from Utica to Clyde), and Western Division (from Clyde to Buffalo). These were self-propelled pump boats, tugs, derrick boats, scows, etc. Their purpose was to minimize delays to canal traffic by pumping out damaged or badly leaking boats and to remove or clear wrecked or sunken boats from the channel as quickly as possible.

There were times when a boat sank in the canal because of a collision or from striking a submerged object. Sometimes a loaded boat sank in the center of the canal, completely blocking the channel. When this happened the nearest wrecking equipment was rushed to the scene, be it day or night. When possible the wreck was given temporary repairs and refloated, but there were times when the wreck had to be torn apart and removed from the channel, so that canal traffic could resume.

A loaded lumber boat was topheavy because of the high deckload; when it sank, it usually capsized, lost its deckload, and righted itself again. The boat would then float, because of the buoyancy of the cargo. Temporary repairs were made, and the boat was then pumped out and the balance of the cargo unloaded at its destination, after which it was drydocked, repaired, and put back in service.

When a boat loaded with pig iron, coal, stone, or gravel sank, the cargo was dredged out of the boat, and a diver was sent down to make temporary repairs. The boat was then pumped out and taken to a drydock.

If a grain boat sank, both the boat and the cargo were usually a total loss. Grain such as wheat, flaxseed, oats, or corn swelled when it got wet and shoved out the side of the boat. The hull split so badly that the cargo had to be dredged out and the boat was dynamited and torn apart piece by piece by the derrick boat to get it out of the channel. Occasionally a boat sank because it had been poorly maintained or because it was too old and worn out. The average life of a wooden canal boat in fresh water was about twenty years unless it was rebuilt.

There were no lights or channel markers along the Erie Canal. A pair of bow lamps, one on each side of the bow deck of the head boat, were standard equipment. If a tow was a triple header, three lights were used, and a lantern was placed between the bow lamps. The number of white lights on the bow of the head boat indicated the number of boats in the tow. The bow lamps were the only help the steersman had to guide the boats at night. They lit up the passing shadowed canal banks, and assisted the steersman in guiding the boats around bends and into the locks. They also warned the locktenders and other boats of an approaching tow.

The only lights on the locks were a white light at each end which let the steersman and driver know they were coming to a lock. The locktender carried a lantern to help find his way around the lock at night.

The bow lamps were a rather bulky affair, being made of metal and glass, and were about sixteen inches square, containing a rather large kerosene lamp and reflectors which lit up the shadowed canal banks. The part containing the kerosene lamp was enclosed in clear glass, as it must stay lit in all kinds of weather.

There were many other articles of equipment required to operate a pair of canal boats, such as hand pumps to keep the bilges free of water, spring poles (which lightened the labor of pumping), pike poles, fenders, tie-up lines, towlines and a horse-bridge for each boat, a set of harnesses for each team, and a set of whiffletrees. Other equipment included lanterns and inside cabin lamps, stoves, dishes, mattresses and bedding, paint brushes, a set of woodworking tools, and caulking tools for repair work. Brooms and shovels were needed to clean the bowstables. There were deck pails with a rope attached to dip up water from the canal and pails for drinking water, also deck boxes, ice chests, and water barrels for the storage of food and drinking water.

Operating equipment included two tiller sticks for each boat. An apparatus to steer the boats when two or more were coupled together, wheel lines or cables, cross lines and windlass-bars were also part of the steering and coupling apparatus. A small and large handwheel to operate the steering gear was also a part of this equipment.

The first forty-six years the canal operated, all or most all the tows were single headers. The boats were steered and controlled by a man at the tiller or rudder. To operate day and night, a single boat required a crew of five—two drivers, two steersmen, and a cook.

In 1871 Fricks Patented Plan of Double Headers was intro-duced on the canal. Two boats were coupled together, one behind the other, and were operated with the same size crew. This plan, and the mechanism to operate it, permitted one man to steer two or three boats coupled together, with less effort and greater pre-cision than could be obtained by a man at the rudder of a single boat.

Old canal men passing the story on said that Frick, a canal driver on a Pennsylvania canal, devised the plan while walking along the towpath. He reasoned that if a suitable steering appara-tus were developed, so that the boats could be kinked or flexed as they approached a bend, the stern boat would act as a rudder for the head boat. His thinking on the subject of steering was entirely correct. The plan was ideal for the animal-powered boats and for the low-powered steam canal boats that first appeared on the canal in 1870. The Frick plan of steering was used on the canal from the time it was introduced until the Erie Canal was abandoned in 1917.

Before and after the new plan of steering was used on the canal, the tows whether light or loaded used long towlines of about 250 feet in length. The long towline gave the steersman better control, as it overcame the tendency of the team to pull the boats toward the towpath, and the method of meeting or passing tows also required a long towline. It was best for pulling the boats from the locks and was necessary when the team crossed over the towpath change bridges without releasing the towline.

The canal boat steering gear was a simple and efficient device, designed so that the boats could be coupled and uncoupled in a few moments. The apparatus was located on the head boat a short distance forward of the cabin. Sturdy and well built, it weighed about 200 pounds and was made of cast iron. It consisted of two flanged 7-inch diameter cable drums about a foot long. The drums were bolted endwise to a cogwheel about 18 inches in diameter which engaged 4-inch sliding pinion gears mounted on a 1¼-inch square shaft. The parts were contained in a suitable frame and operated by a steersman at a 4-foot diameter spoked hand wheel. Turning the hand wheel played out one cable and took in the other, so as to allow the rear boat to change its alignment with the front boat.

The unit stood on four legs, which were bolted to the deck. Cables 5/8-inch in diameter led from the drums to sheaves on the outside edge of the head boat and followed back to sheaves on the outside edge of the stern boat's bow. The cables were led around the rear boat's sheaves and were fastened to a cleat on the stern of the head boat. The rear boat had a 10-inch square wooden fender about 3 feet long, which hung from a center cleat over the bow and kept the boats 10 inches apart when they were coupled together by a pair of cross lines attached to the head boat. These crossed lines ran through chocks or sheaves to a double drum windlass on the rear boat, which enabled the boatman to rachet the boats tightly together. The crossed lines kept the boats perfectly in line with each other and allowed them to pivot on the bow fender, around bends or sharp turns in the canal. This steering arrangement gave the steersman excellent control of the boats when towed by animal power at the slow speed of from one to 2½ miles an hour. Even at these slow speeds, steersmen were sometimes injured by the spinning spoke handles if the wheel was pulled from their hands because of an extra strong tension on the steering cables, when the boats began swinging too fast while rounding a sharp bend. When this occurred, steersmen had to let go and step clear of the spinning wheel. Some steersmen were injured by holding on to the wheel too long in these situations, and some were thrown over the top of the 4-foot handwheel. Injuries became more common when steam power came on the Old Erie Canal.

On grain boats the steering gear was bolted permanently to the deck. On lumber boats it was bolted to a movable platform which spanned the open cargo hold, in front of the boat's cabin, when the boat was light or empty. To enable the steersman to see over the 7-foot high deckload on a lumber boat, when the head boat was being loaded, the steering gear on its platform was set atop the cabin. When the deck load reached a certain height, the gear and platform were lagscrewed to the cargo, directly above its former position on the boat. Extra sheaves and snatch blocks were then used to run the steering cables in proper alignment with the rear boat's sheaves.

Many canal boat steering gears were manufactured by the Gillie Foundry and Machine Company in Tonawanda. The Gillie name was also on many sheaves, chocks, cleats, iron ventilator covers, and windlasses.

CHAPTER 6

Hudson River Boating

DEPARTING from Tonawanda in midsummer, with two boat loads of lumber consigned to the Steinway piano factory in Brooklyn, we made a trip over the Erie Canal and down the Hudson River to New York City that I recall with much pleasure.

The return trip to Tonawanda I remember in greater detail than most of the early trips. I suppose it was because we usually went back empty, but this time we took on a cargo for the return trip.

It was 1909. I was six in August and was then old enough to be a wide-eyed and interested observer of everything, from the time we were put in the Hudson River tow at Albany, until we returned there eight days later. The steersman had been laid off when we arrived at Albany. My Uncle Charles, Mother's younger brother who was driving our mules that summer, was put in charge of the head boat. My father and mother, and my older brother Jim, myself, a younger sister, and a baby brother were on the second boat, the *Sol Goldsmith.* Before the start of a tow down the Hudson it was necessary to assemble and make up the tow as the canal boats arrived at Albany. I was told by older boatmen that in the early days when canal shipping was very busy, the tows were made up on the Albany and Rensselaer side of the river, but in my day they were made up only on the Rensselaer side of the river below the bridges. This eliminated the risk of the large tow striking the Albany-Rensselaer bridge piers when starting down the river. Nor did it interfere with the Albany harbor traffic while being assembled.

Once the tow was under way it was a period of relaxation for the boatmen. No steersmen were needed, since the tugs guided the boats. There would be no locks to pass through or time spent caring for animals as the teams were let out to pasture in the Albany vicinity until the boats returned from New York. Only the lines holding the boats together were to be inspected and kept tight. The boats would be kept pumped out, and that was it until the tow reached New York. This would take about 48 hours. Many of the boatmen did odd jobs, such as splicing lines, caulking, painting decks and cabin tops, and handling other small repair jobs. They also visited back and forth. I enjoyed going with Father when he visited other boatmen in tow, because I liked to hear them talk of other canal men they knew, and to hear them tell of things that had happened to them while going up and down the canal.

My first visit with him aboard a "Bum Boat" that came out to the tow opposite Kingston was a very satisfying event, for I never expected to be eating fresh ice cream, purchased going down the middle of the Hudson River.

The Bum Boats sold—at regular retail prices to the boatmen— fresh meats, baked goods, eggs, soft drinks, candy, ice cream, and other such commodities. Coming alongside, it hooked onto our tow while the boatmen went aboard and bought what they wanted, including cold bottled beer.

The small canopied Bum Boats were steam powered. They stayed alongside until we met another river tow going in the opposite direction. Leaving us, they tied onto the other tow and returned to their starting point. They "bummed" a tow from a fleet going down the river and up the river; hence the name *Bum Boat.*

During the daylight hours I spent most of my time sitting on top of the cabin, watching the shoreline of the Hudson and asking questions about the towns and scenes along the river or watching the busy shuttle tug. I always remembered the bridges crossing the river at Poughkeepsie, and was told that this was the halfway point between Albany and New York City. No matter what was going on I always kept my eyes and ears open for the Bum Boats and other craft plying the river.

When our tow arrived at New York I was amazed at the never-ending flow of harbor traffic. There were tugs pushing car floats loaded with freight cars back and forth from Manhattan to New Jersey. I saw steam-propelled lighters with a long forward deck and a derrick mounted forward of the pilot house. They were used for transferring small lots of freight from the piers to steamships; there were self-propelled, steam-powered, floating elevators

for transferring grain directly from canal boats and barges into the steamship's cargo holds. I saw tugs towing or pushing covered deck barges for transferring package freight and open deck barges for handling bulk freight. Last of all, there were the busy double-ended passenger ferry boats shuttling back and forth across the harbor.

Dump scows and garbage scows were being towed to sea. Ocean-going freighters were anchored in the river waiting to be docked at a pier. I liked to watch the tugs docking the huge passenger liners at the North River piers. These were all sights I never tired of watching. Anything afloat always had my full attention.

The type of large river tow that landed us at New York came to an end soon after the Erie Canal was abandoned. The opening of the Barge Canal ended the animal power that was used on the Erie. Each Barge Canal fleet had its own towboat that also towed them on the Hudson River after they were out of the canal.

After unloading the lumber for the Steinway piano factory in Brooklyn, we were towed to the canal piers on South Street at the foot of Manhattan Island. Here we waited a few days for orders from an agent who was to secure loads for our boats for the return trip to Tonawanda.

Although I was quite young and had been to New York City before, this time I was old enough to remember our stay at the canal piers on South Street. My brother Jim, who was almost two years older than I, was entrusted to take me sightseeing along the busy streets bordering the waterfront. We visited the nearby Fulton Street fish market, a very busy place, and strolled by the stalls amazed by all the different kinds of saltwater fish brought in by the fishing fleet. We walked back along bustling South Street, which was always a beehive of activity due to the arrival and departure of the many tugs, barges, and other kinds of vessel traffic. Most of the business places along here catered to waterfront customers. In this area there were many push-carts selling all kinds of merchandise and food. We bought fresh oysters and clams on the half shell for a penny apiece. Hot dogs were a nickel (they were called Coney Island red hots), and many other items of ready-to-eat food and candy could be found at prices only to be had along the waterfront.

Within walking distance of where our boats lay was the old circular red brick building that housed the New York City Aquarium in Battery Park. Here, for the first time, we saw many types of saltwater fish swimming in glass tanks. There were seahorses, dolphins, seals, octopi, swordfish, striped bass, and many other forms of saltwater marine life. This building has since been removed, and the aquarium is now housed in modern buildings at Coney Island.

That evening we were told that two loads of fine white sea gravel consigned to the Ayrault Roofing Company in Tonawanda had been secured for the return trip west. Early the next morning, a small steam tug hooked on to our two empty boats and towed us up the East River, then through the Hell Gate. After a few hours' tow on Long Island Sound we arrived at Oyster Bay and were moored at the gravel dock, ready to load. Two days later we were back at the South Street piers waiting to be placed in the next westbound Hudson River tow.

The view from South Street took in many of the sights that were mentioned in our school history and geography books. We could see the Brooklyn Bridge, the skyscrapers of lower Manhattan, and the Statue of Liberty on Bedloe Island. Also Governor's Island and a U.S. military reservation that had its own Government ferry running to and from the mainland. Busy double-ended ferry boats were shuttling back and forth from Manhattan to Brooklyn and to Staten Island. These, with other busy harbor traffic, were all in plain view from our canal boats.

Toward evening a harbor tug towed us up the North River, where we were placed in the Cornell tow being made up opposite 52nd street. The tow was tied to what was called the "stake boat," anchored in the middle of the river. The anchored boats would swing around with the tide when it ran in or out. Tie-up lines stayed tight as the anchored boats rose and fell with the tide. The boatmen now had to stay aboard their boats until the tow reached its destination.

Early the next morning we started for Albany. Soon after we were under way we were passing by Riverside Park, where the well-known landmark Grant's Tomb could be seen close to the shoreline. Next we passed Spuyten Duyvil Creek, which separates the northern end of Manhattan Island from the mainland. The creek was named "Spitting Devil" by the early Dutch settlers because of the violent cross-currents and eddies which occurred when the tide was running in or out.

Twelve miles or so from New York we came to the beginning of the Palisades, a series of rocky cliffs that extend for miles along the New Jersey shore on the west side of the river. Resembling tall columns or pillars, they are from 350 to 500 feet in height, an imposing and majestic sight to view while moving slowly up the Hudson. The Palisades ended in Rockland County, New York, but on the way we had passed Yonkers, Dobbs Ferry, Tarrytown, and the village of Rockland Lake.

One of my earliest recollections of the Hudson River was the time we were put in a Hudson tow and dropped off at Rockland Lake, soon after we had unloaded lumber in Brooklyn. The village is on the west shore of the Hudson about twenty-eight miles from New York. Here we loaded crushed stone for an upstate road-building job. The crushed stone from Rockland Lake was highly valued as a base for good roads. Canal boats carried the stone to many places in the state. Some of it went as far west as Seneca Falls, where it was used for a road-building job between that town and Waterloo.

While waiting to load on that earlier trip, I remember a warm evening we all went swimming in the Hudson. The bathing party included our family and a young woman named Clara, a guest and friend of my mother from Tonawanda, who had come along for a pleasure trip. While we were all swimming, it was mentioned how much easier it was to swim and float in salt water. What I remember best was my Dad paddling around with me on his back, as I had not yet learned to swim.

In the early 1900s five stone crushers were in operation at the busy quarry. The quarrying of stone from the Palisades was a most economical operation. A few sticks of dynamite, set off at the base of the cliffs, caused large amounts of stone to fall in the laps of the quarrymen. Eventually, in the interest of conservation, the Palisades Interstate Park Commission must have been successful in obtaining the land in the Rockland Lake area and closed the quarries. We never stopped there after the one trip, and I don't recall what year boating stone from Rockland Lake ended.

About three miles north of Rockland Lake we passed the small city of Ossining on the east shore of the river. Set back some distance inland we could see the towers and roofs of Sing Sing Prison. In those days, even to a young boy it was an awesome place, for it was there that many hardened criminals and murderers were put to death in Sing Sing's notorious electric chair.

Leaving Ossining we continued on across Haverstraw Bay, which is quite wide, and we could see the city of Haverstraw spread out on the distant western shoreline. Next, just before entering the Narrows, was Peekskill, where the normally wide Hudson narrowed going through the Highlands. At this point the lofty peaks of the Appalachians end abruptly on the shores of the river. Then we passed the old and famous West Point Military Academy, which is in plain view on its lofty site on the west shore of the river.

Next came the city of Beacon on the east shore of the river, and on the opposite shore, the old and picturesque city of Newburgh. The whole city was in plain view of the tow as we moved slowly along the river. During the Revolutionary war years of 1782-1783, General Washington made his headquarters in Newburgh at the Hasbrouck House, dating from 1725, which is now a national shrine maintained by the State.

After Newburgh came Poughkeepsie, the halfway point between Albany and New York City. At this point a high-level railroad bridge crossed to Highland on the west shore of the river.

Here also was the mid-river highway bridge. These were the only bridges crossing the Hudson River between Albany and New York City in the early 1900s.

A nationally famous product was born in Poughkeepsie. In 1841, the Smith Brothers started an ice cream parlor and candy business there, which eventually became the start of the well-known Smith Brothers cough drops.

The next place of interest was the entrance to Rondout Creek, marked by a lighthouse called the Esopus Light. It served as a guide for tows entering the Creek at night and for tows and other vessels passing up and down the river. The old landmark, sixty miles from Albany, was once a reminder for boatmen that this was the best place along the river to fill up the drinking water barrels and freshwater tanks.

The water was fresh and clean after flowing from its source high up in the Adirondacks. If one attempted to fill up with water below Esopus Light, it could be contaminated with salt water, which had flowed up the river with the incoming tide. Today, pollution in the water would make this practice of getting fresh water impossible.

The famous old side wheel steamer *Mary Powell,* the "queen of the river," lay idle at Rondout, her home port, for a few years before being scrapped. I saw her lying there in 1920 when towing a fleet of barges down the Hudson. Holding the speed record on the river for many years, she was long and low in the water without much superstructure. The white paint then weathered, and the twin black smoke stacks rusting away, she seemed to be quietly waiting for her last voyage, which would be to the wrecking yard. When slowly passing up the Hudson in a river tow it was always a pleasing sight to see the large passenger boats that ran between New York and Albany. When they met or passed tows on the river, you could see the spray and foam rising from the side wheels and hear the noise of the paddles as they slapped the water. On the top deck, one could see the walking beam that connected the boat's engines to the paddle wheels, constantly rising up and down, driving the boat forward and creating a huge swell as it neared the tow.

These swells always brought forth a few cuss words from the canal and bargemen, because they made the tow heave and surge, sometimes breaking the towlines. When passing a tow, the passenger boats always slowed down some, but never enough to suit the men in charge of the tow.

After dark, as the passenger boats approached our tow, we could see their powerful searchlights shining and darting from one side of the river to the other, looking for buoys, or other boats in the channel. If it was early in the evening they were lit up like a small city as they passed by.

The Hudson River passenger boats were called "The Dayline" and "The Nightline." A Dayline boat left Albany and New York each morning and arrived at New York and Albany each evening. The Nightline boats left Albany and New York each evening and arrived at their destinations the next morning.

In the summer of 1921 I rode the night boat from New York to Albany. It was a ten-hour trip. The fare, which included a stateroom, was $6. The Hudson River passenger boats were very large vessels, three or four decks high, painted white, with from one to three smokestacks. They did a thriving business from the 1880s to the early 1900s. They have stopped running now, as have the passenger vessels on the Great Lakes.

When we reached Kingston, we were no longer in salt water. The natural current in the Hudson River kept the tide from carrying the salt water any farther upstream. From Kingston almost to Albany, the shores of the river were dotted with wooden ice houses, which were filled each winter when the river had frozen over. During the season of navigation the ice was shipped by special barges to New York City. Electric refrigeration was a long way off when these ice houses were built. The ice barges were picked up and dropped off at the various ice houses by the same large tows that handled the canal boats on the river. The ice houses and barges belonged to the Knickerbocker Ice Co. The deck house and cabin of the barges were painted bright yellow, and the hull or lower part was light gray color. Each barge had a windmill mounted on top of the cabin, which powered a bilge pump that kept the barge free of melting ice and bilge water. Not many barge captains would stay on a boat where they had to strain their backs, working a hand pump every spare moment.

The company's name and the windmill mounted on a ten-foot-high tower atop the covered ice barge's after cabin always made me think of Holland. There are a few of these old ice houses still standing, even though it's a long time since any ice has been harvested on the river. Those left standing are used to raise mushrooms, which flourish in the old sawdust that was used to insulate the ice.

After leaving Kingston, the next point of interest was the village of Catskill on the west shore of the river. Not too far away is the scene of the legendary twenty-year sleep of Rip Van Winkle. While passing here, we encountered a summer storm. There was lightning, and crashes of thunder echoed from the mountains. Mother wondered if the thunder was caused by the game of ten pins dreamed of by Rip in his long sleep. You can believe that we children were all ears when we heard this and that we always remembered this village on the Hudson River.

The next large cities along the river after leaving Catskill were Hudson on the east shore and Athens on the opposite side. Hudson was high on the shoreline and in plain view of our tow. There were the usual double-ended ferry boats shuttling across the river between the two cities. Athens was easily identified by the white smoke coming from the tall chimneys of a large cement plant.

The next point of interest was Coxsackie, another river town; then came Castleton-on-Hudson, just ten miles south of Albany. This was the second place that a bridge *would* be built across the Hudson River. After passing the city of Hudson on the north shore of the river, the valley widened and the river narrowed, becoming low marshland as we approached Albany and Rensselaer, which were on opposite sides of the Hudson.

This was the destination of the large tow which had consisted of many types of barges and canal boats when it had left New

York City forty-eight hours earlier. By the time we arrived at Albany, the tow consisted mostly of canal boats. Along the river we had dropped off ice and sand barges, brick, stone, and cement barges, and some barges to be repaired at the Rondout and Kingston boatyards. At that time many of the industries along the river used different types of barges to ship their products to New York City.

The bulk of the tow had been made up of Erie, Champlain, and a few Black River canal boats. At Albany the tow was broken up and smaller tugs dropped the boats off at different docks or the canal locks at Albany or Watervliet. Canal boats moving westward usually avoided locking up into the Erie Canal at Albany because of the congestion in the Albany lumber district. Lumber boats would be unloading there on each side of the canal.

Whenever we were leaving or passing Albany, our parents would point out the red-tiled roofs and towers of the State Capitol Building on Capitol Hill. The State Capitol stood out clearly from the river, as our boats moved upstream in tow of a small Cornell tug headed for the canal lock at Watervliet. Opposite Watervliet is the city of Troy, seven or eight miles upriver from Albany and the last tidewater city on the Hudson. Troy is the seat of Rensselaer County and, among other industries, is noted for the manufacture of men's shirts and collars. Troy's leadership in this industry is credited to a Troy housewife, Hannah (Mrs. Orlando) Montague, who in 1819 devised detachable collars for her husband's shirts. From that point on, Troy became known as "The Collar City."

CHAPTER 7

From Albany to Rome

W E COULD NOT see every village, town, city, and other point of interest along the canal on one trip. The boats operated day and night, and we would be sleeping when passing through many of them. What was missed on one trip, though, would be seen on another. We liked to be on deck when passing through the villages, towns, or cities, as the activities of the people and the traffic was interesting and exciting to a youngster. At that time the traffic consisted mostly of street cars and horse-drawn wagons or buggies and bicycles.

At Watervliet, our boats were locked up into the Erie Canal from the Hudson River. Watervliet is the home of the United States' oldest arsenal, established in 1813. Here, many types of antiaircraft armament and battleship ordnance were still being manufactured by the government in World War II. On our arrival in Watervliet we picked up our mules, which had been pastured out at a nearby farm while we made the trip to and from New York City. We then started on our long haul up the Erie Canal with our two partly loaded boats, drawing four feet of water.

We soon came to the busy manufacturing city of Cohoes, where we started to climb from the Hudson River Valley up to the Mohawk Valley, a rise of 169 feet. The ascent from the Hudson was accomplished by means of sixteen single-twinned locks. The single locks were abreast of each other. One was used for upbound boats and the other for downbound. They were a short way apart, and spaced over a distance of three and a half miles. As we neared the top of the "sixteens," we could look back and see the canal and the locks winding their way down the side of the valley. This was—and remains today—one of the most attractive and scenic spots on the canal.

On arriving at the "sixteens," the two boats were separated to save time and the labor of uncoupling and coupling up the boats at each lock. Another team was hired, and the boats were towed singly over the short levels. When we arrived at the top of the flight of locks, the extra driver and team were paid off, and the boats were again coupled together. Our own tired team was put aboard the boats, and the fresh and rested team was put on the towpath.

Men who owned canal teams were stationed at Cohoes. They made a living assisting canal fleets through the sixteen locks. All the boatmen singled up the boats here because of the single locks and short levels. The extra team was hired to save overworking their own animals and to shorten the time required to pass through sixteen locks. The canal continued a short distance along the south side of the Mohawk River to a point opposite the small village of Crescent, so named because of the shape of the river at that location. Here we crossed the river on the longest aqueduct on the canal (1,137 feet). The canal then followed along the north shore of the river for 12 miles to Rexford Flats. Here the canal recrossed the river to the south side on another long aqueduct (610 feet), and then headed for Schenectady, where the General Electric Company had its huge factories and laboratories, the largest of their kind in the world. They were established in 1886.

Arriving at Schenectady we were entering and about to travel through the most historic section of the Mohawk Valley. We would pass the sites of a number of old forts, battlefields, and villages which figured prominently in our early history. At Schenectady, the Dutch had built a fort in 1695, and the construction of some of the houses still shows the Dutch influence today. The name Schenectady was probably derived from the Indian word *Schonowe*, "the place-beyond-the-pine-plains," and it was conceded that the Indians meant it was the gateway to the west. There was very little attempt at navigating the Mohawk between Schenectady and Cohoes Falls because of the swift current and hazards in the river.

The Erie Canal's 610-foot-long aqueduct crossing the Mohawk River at Rexford Flats, N.Y. The men on the left are walking on the aqueduct towpath. The upper aqueduct Lock 20 is a few hundred feet beyond the north end of this aqueduct. *Buffalo and Erie County Historical Society.*

After leaving Schenectady we passed by the villages of Scotia, Rotterdam, and Cranesville. Three miles farther on would put us opposite the city of Amsterdam on the north shore of the Mohawk. This city was noted for its manufacture and production of rugs and carpets, which began in 1837. It also was once the largest manufacturer of brooms and pearl buttons of any city in the world and known for its output of knit goods, linseed oil, and paper products. In 1906 the Amsterdam Board of Trade reported that the Fonda, Johnstown, and Gloversville Railroad carried 3,888,198 passengers for the year ending June 30, 1905, and that it was the seventh longest trolley line in New York State.

The name of the city of Amsterdam reminds me of the first Dutch settlers, whose influence in the development of New York State began at Manhattan Island and spread up the Hudson River and Mohawk Valley as far west as the city of Fonda and the villages of Yost and Sprakers, which I believe are named from the descendants of the first Dutch people who came to America. Amsterdam would still be in sight as we passed slowly through the village of Port Jackson on the opposite shore of the Mohawk River.

View of Lock 21, with a pair of loaded eastbound grain boats passing through the lock. This lock was a short distance east of the 610-foot-long aqueduct that carried the canal across the Mohawk River at Rexford, N.Y., a few miles east of Schenectady. Note horse bridge on bowstable and drinking-water barrel in center of hatches. Photo *circa* early 1900s. *Buffalo and Erie County Historical Society.*

This is an elevated and different view of Lock 21—known as the lower aqueduct lock—a highway bridge, and the towpath. It was about 1500 feet east of Lock 22—known as the upper aqueduct lock. Both locks were on the north shore of the Mohawk River, this one a short distance from Rexford, N.Y. Photo *circa* early 1900s. *Buffalo and Erie County Historical Society.*

A mile west of Port Jackson on the north shore of the river, near the outskirts of Amsterdam, one could see Guy Park Mansion. It was built in 1766 by Sir William Johnson as a wedding present for his nephew Guy Johnson, who married Sir William's daughter Mary.

A short distance west of the Guy Park Mansion on the opposite side of the road is the site of Fort Johnson. A handsome gray stone mansion on this site was the home of Sir William Johnson before he built Johnson Hall at Johnstown, New York. Four or five miles farther on we came to the site of Fort Hunter; nearby was the site of Queen Anne's Church, a stone edifice built for the Indians. In the path of the first canal, it was torn down, and the stones from the church were used to build a guard lock near the church site on the edge of Schoharie Creek. A short distance from here, we crossed the sometimes turbulent Schoharie Creek, on a stone-arched wooden trunk aqueduct 640 feet long. The creek was very wide here, where it emptied into the Mohawk River. Still there at Fort Hunter on the east side of Schoharie Creek, in fair condition, is the first Erie Canal guard lock built in 1822 by the builders of the Grand Canal.

Here a dam was built across the creek raising it to canal level. The creek then served as a feeder for the canal. The guard lock was used when the creek rose above normal level. Many boats were damaged or sunk when attempting to cross the creek when it was at flood stage.

By 1841 a new and enlarged canal channel had been constructed about a thousand feet north of the first Erie; and an aqueduct was built to carry the canal traffic across Schoharie Creek, which made the crossing there a routine matter during high water.

A few miles west of Fort Hunter, we could see the Auriesville Shrine high up on the south side of the hill overlooking the valley. The shrine marks the site where Indians murdered the three French missionaries, Father Isaac Jouges and Brothers Rene Goupil and Jean Lalande in the 1640s. The shrine was established in 1885 in honor of these and five other priests. The 72-door Coliseum on its 700-acre setting draws people from all over the world. The shrine is administered by the Jesuit Fathers.

The next village we passed through was Fultonville, named in honor of Robert Fulton. On the opposite or north side of the Mohawk River was the village of Fonda. By the time the first canal opened, the village of Fultonville was well established, having a store, a flour mill, a distillery, a paper mill, an ashery, a sawmill, a blacksmith shop, and other small industries. Sometime later a grain elevator was built on the edge of the Erie to handle canal shipments.

Even though the canal did not pass through Fonda, this seat of Montgomery County was well known to canallers. Anyone mentioning the name of this Mohawk Valley town usually brought a smile to the face of the sober and industrious segment of canallers. For it was well known that quite a number of drivers and

The 15-foot wide by 90-foot long Empire Lock, one mile east of Fort Hunter, N.Y. It was built in 1822 as a section of the first Erie Grand Canal channel. *Buffalo and Erie County Historical Society.*

steersmen, who had drunk up their season's earnings, would head for Fonda when the canal closed in the fall. Here they hoped to be jailed on a vagrancy charge for the winter. It was said that a fee was received from the county for each prisoner lodged in jail. The vagrants were fed and allowed tobacco money and were permitted to go into town during the week. The canal men were conveniently discharged about the time the Erie was to open in the spring, with a clean and well-fed look about them when they showed up at the canal towns at the start of the season.

A few hours after leaving Fultonville we came to one of the most scenic places along the valley, called "the Noses." At this spot it looks as though the Mohawk River had carved its way through the Appalachian Mountain chain. No doubt the breach was made during the ice age, and the result is an opening in the mountain chain. Close to the north shore, Big Nose rises in a steep slope 640 feet above the river and is covered with many evergreen trees. The dark foliage is in contrast with the lighter greens of oak and maple found on most of the hills and mountains in the valley. The historic Mohawk Trail is near the edge of the river as it passes around Big Nose on the river's north shore. Farther away from the river's edge on the south side, Little Nose rock rises on a more gradual slope to 740 feet.

This hill on the south side of the river seems to be misnamed, since it is higher than Big Nose on the north-shore side of the Mohawk. Near its top, a little distance to the south, is the egg-shaped opening of Mitchell's cavern, the entrance to which must be made by a perpendicular drop, by means of a rope, of about 16 feet to an 11 x 30-foot opening. From this point by inclined plane and perpendicular descent, Perry N. Van Epps and others once penetrated to a depth of 280 feet without finding any large rooms or extensive horizontal galleries. The cavern has the appearance of having been formed by a huge cleft in the mountain, and any exploration is made not without some danger, and with considerable · discomfort.

We soon came to lock 31 in the small village of Sprakers, so named for an early settler who established a huge canal store there. Open night and day, it stocked everything for man or beast and canal boats. We paused here for awhile until we replenished our drinking water, groceries, and other supplies.

Our progress with the partly loaded boats was slow as we were steadily rising up through the valley. The levels and the distance between the locks were short, and there were occasional delays when we met other canal fleets at the locks; but this type of delay was common.

Ahead was the town of Canajoharie, where we crossed a short aqueduct over Baumen's Creek. The town is well known for its food-processing industry and especially the Beech Nut plants located between the canal and the Mohawk River. This town has an aboriginal name which was first given by the Mohawks to the creek flowing through the area. The creek was so named from a remarkable natural phenomenon connected with it. Nearly three-fourths of a mile from the junction of the creek with the Mohawk River was a hole in the rocky bed of the river, averaging more than twenty feet in diameter, with a depth of about ten feet. This cavity, resembling a large cistern, was formerly nearly round with vertical walls, but within the last quarter century its rim has become broken down and the side toward the current of the creek somewhat elongated. This singular excavation made in the course of ages by the action of the water and rolling stones was called by the Indians "the pot that washes itself," which is how the village of Canajoharie got its name.

On the north shore of the Mohawk opposite Canajoharie is the village of Palatine Bridge, founded in 1723 by early German settlers who had come to America to escape religious persecution in their homeland. Three miles farther on we came to the village of Fort Plain, which is located a half-mile or so east of the site of the old fort that dates back to 1738; this fort was prominent in the early wars between the British, French, and Indians. A few miles westward we could see St. Johnsville, an old mill town on the north shore of the Mohawk River.

Next we crossed an aqueduct over Castle Creek; nearby was Indian Castle Church, erected in 1769. A few miles on we passed a red brick farmhouse that was within a few hundred feet of the canal. This was the home of General Nicholas Herkimer, built in 1764. The house overlooks the canal and the Mohawk from its site on the south shore of the river. It was here that the hero of the Battle of Oriskany died from a wound suffered in the enemy ambush. The resting place of the General, marked by a tall imposing monument, is a short distance from the red brick house. Now a national shrine, the house and grounds are maintained by New York State. Still in view from the house today is an old stone bridge abutment on the edge of the abandoned Erie Canal bed.

Two miles west of the General Herkimer house we came to the city of Little Falls. Passing through four locks we were raised above the sometimes turbulent waters of the falls. On our way through the city we passed by what remained of a shallow, earlier Erie Canal aqueduct that was once part of a side cut that conveyed boats to a canal basin on the north side of the Mohawk River in the village of Little Falls. It is shallow because it was built for the first Erie Canal boats of three-and-a-half foot draft, and is constructed of solid masonry. The Little Falls side cut was abandoned a few years after the enlargement of the original canal was com-

pleted in 1862. But the old aqueduct that was once a part of the
side cut is still straddling the river with one of its arches destroyed,
and it remains a longstanding reminder of DeWitt Clinton's "Grand
Canal."

About ten miles westward we passed through the busy manufacturing towns of Mohawk, Ilion, and Frankfort. The three towns
were strung out closely together along the canal, so that it seemed
as we left one we entered the other. Opposite the village of Mohawk, the city of Herkimer on the north side of the river was built
on the site of Fort Dayton, an early settlement, once called German Flats. We next passed through the busy town of Ilion, where
the huge Remington Arms plant, established in 1826, is located.
The foundation wall of one of the long red brick buildings served
as a berm on the south side of the canal. When our slow-moving
boats were passing by, I could look in the open windows of the
factory and see the belt-driven machinery turning out parts. When
orders for arms were slow, Remington diversified its manufacture,
and in 1856 began turning out agricultural implements. After
1870 it began producing sewing machines as well as firearms.

Gone are the weary drivers behind the plodding mules that
towed the slow-moving canal boats. Gone are the old-time steersmen, who, like the drivers, stayed out in the open, guiding the
boats night and day in all kinds of weather. Gone and filled in is
the outmoded Erie Canal that once passed through Ilion. But
nothing seems to interrupt the manufacture of firearms, for the
busy Remington Arms plants are still there along the filled-in
canal bed.

Passing from Ilion into Frankfort we were on the lookout for any activity at the Frankfort drydock. Frankfort was an industrial village settled in 1723, and, viewed from the canal, it was a quiet country village. In 1840 the first bridge in America, made of iron throughout, was built by Earl Trumbull over the Erie Canal at Frankfort. This bridge of cast iron girders was strengthened by wrought-iron rods.

Next, our canal boats passed through Utica, a busy city noted for its textile industries, knitting mills, clothing factories, and many other products. Whenever we passed through Utica, I was always on deck to see if any canal boats were unloading sand at the old foundry along the canal bank. The foundry received its sand shipments by canal for a good many years, although I don't recall any canal boats regularly engaged in hauling sand to Utica. It was usually carried by canal boats that had unloaded cargoes in the New York City area; some of them were then towed up the Raritan River to New Brunswick, N.J., where they loaded the molding sand for Utica. After the boats were unloaded at Utica they continued on to Tonawanda or Buffalo, where they again took on cargoes to carry back east.

The unloading rig at the foundry was a crude, stiff-leg derrick built of unfinished logs. A simple mast supported a boom that was swung out over the boat by a man pulling on a rope attached to the end of the boom; the boom was swung ashore the same way. A 500-pound capacity bucket was lowered into the boat, where four men then shoveled it full of sand. The power to raise and lower the bucket was supplied by a single horse, an animal so used to the job that no driver was needed. The man who swung the boom and dumped the bucket simply told the horse when to go ahead and when to back up. The weight of the bucket on the lift rope kept the whiffletree free of the horse's heels when the animal backed up. The faithful horse made 400 trips ahead and back to unload each 100-ton boatload of sand coming to that foundry.

Utica was a busy place indeed, and there were many things to see as we passed slowly through the city; but the unloading of the sand boats is the one I remember best.

We came to the village of Oriskany next, and here we crossed Oriskany Creek on an aqueduct 105 feet long. Crossing an aqueduct was always interesting, because, as we slowly crossed, it gave us an elevated view of the countryside bordering the stream. Nine miles west of Utica we passed close by the Oriskany Battlefield; a tall monument marks the site where, on August 4, 1777, General Herkimer and his valiant army were ambushed by the British and Indians, and American patriots forced the enemy to retreat.

A few miles westward from the monument we came to the city of Rome, which was a terminus and the beginning of the Black River Canal. This canal followed the Black River north through Boonville and Lyons Falls to Carthage. Begun in 1836, it was not completely finished until 1855. Most of the freight carried on the canal was forest and farm products from the North Country area. It was never profitable and its usefulness dwindled in the 1870s when the railroads became more established in that area.

The Black River Canal was never enlarged or improved. The locks were still the original size, 15 x 90 feet when it closed. The 75-ton boats carried about a third of the tonnage of boats such as ours, which were built for the enlarged Erie Canal. They were almost miniature in size when compared with Erie boats. Until the early 1900s, these small boats occasionally transferred or picked up cargoes from Erie Canal boats here at Rome, but they also carried cargoes to and from Buffalo, as well as to and from New York City. I recall seeing them in the large Hudson River tows with cargoes for New York. Although it was never a financial success, the Black River Canal was the longest-used of the unimproved lateral canals. This was because it was a feeder needed to maintain the water supply for the lower long level between Utica and Syracuse. The Black River Canal was abandoned in 1923.

The city of Rome is the seat of Oneida County. The heart of the Mohawk Valley Basin, the land is flat and level for miles, and the muckland in this area yields large crops of onions and other farm produce. Rome is also known for its copper and brass products. The Revere Copper and Brass rolling mills are located here, and Revere is the largest employer in the city. The company was named for Paul Revere, who built the first foundry and rolling mill for the production of copper in America. Many tons of copper slabs or pigs were hauled to Rome for this company in Erie Canal boats. The site of the city played an important part in the early wars in America and in the history of transportation in New York State.

CHAPTER 8

From Utica to Lock Berlin

S LOWLY LEAVING the Mohawk Valley behind, we continued over the lower long level, which stretched fifty-six miles from Lock 46 at Utica to Lock 47 at Syracuse. This was the second longest level on the Erie Canal.

After leaving Rome, we passed through a number of small towns and villages. New London was first; then Grove Springs, no longer there; Stacy's Basin and Higginsville, which was once the terminus of the Oneida Lake Canal.

The first Oneida Lake Canal extended from the Erie Canal at Higginsville to Wood Creek and then to Oneida Lake. Its total length was 6½ miles. This canal was built for the purpose of opening vast tracts of timber lands in the region of the canal and Oneida Lake. Navigation opened in September 1885. The original canal was built by a private company and purchased by the State in 1841; but due to lack of commerce, dilapidated structures, and a neglected channel, it was not used after 1862. A different route was chosen for a new Oneida Lake Canal, to run from Durhamville on the Erie Canal to South Bay on Oneida Lake.

Started in 1866, it was not completed until October 1877. This new, short 5½-mile canal had a brief existence. Poorly planned and constructed, it encountered many mishaps, largely due to breaks in the canal's banks. There was always a danger of its rupturing and draining the Erie Canal. Its usefulness having diminished, it was consequently abandoned in 1887.

77

Will Doran's Erie Canal boatyard and drydock at Durhamville, N.Y. The new canal boat *Alfred E. Smith* is being launched. This was an animal-drawn grain boat with a Tonawanda-type scow bow. Photo *circa* early 1900s.

Durhamville is a small town, and in 1909 it had a drydock and boatyard where many Erie Canal boats were built. I heard the name of the boat builder mentioned many times by my father and other canal men. Will Doran was always spoken of favorably: he must have extended credit and good terms to those who did business with him. The village, about three miles north of the city of Oneida, has a street named Doran, which I always assumed was named in honor of the boat builder.

Next we passed through Canastota, Chittenango, and Manlius Center. DeWitt, on the outskirts of Syracuse, was next. Here, at Lock 47, was the western end of the 56-mile level which began near Utica. The three locks in the city descended west toward Onondaga Lake and the Oswego River watershed, as the Erie Canal route went westward to Rochester and Lake Ontario.

We were always on deck when passing through Syracuse, for there were many interesting things to see in the "Salt City." The canal went through Syracuse near the heart of the city. At that time, the railroad ran through this busy place at street level, caus-

Will Doran's Erie Canal boatyard and drydock, Durhamville, N.Y., with a new canal boat about ready for launching. The bowstable indicates this is another animal-drawn boat with a laker type bow. A steam yacht or excursion boat is in the drydock to the right. Photo *circa* early 1900s.

ing delays and traffic tie-ups, as, of course, did the canal also. A number of bridges crossing the canal were lift bridges that had to be raised for us to pass under. We could see the traffic held up in long lines waiting for our boats to pass by. The traffic at that time consisted of street cars, horses and wagons, and pedestrians. The bridges were operated by water power, for electric power was not available for this purpose in 1909.

A familiar sight was the old Greek-styled Weighlock Building, erected in 1850. The north side of the building extended over the weighlock and housed the scale used to calculate the amount of tolls on boat cargoes in early canal operations. When canal tolls were abolished at the end of the 1881 canal season, the weighlock was kept operative for inspecting state canal equipment. In an emergency it was sometimes used as a drydock for making tempo-rary repairs to damaged or badly leaking canal boats. The weigh-lock building continued to be used for Barge Canal System offices, and later the building housed New York State Administrative offices. Today it is home of the Canal Museum.

On the north side of the canal, almost opposite the Weighlock Building, was the junction of the Oswego Canal and the Erie. Running northerly for 38 miles, the Oswego Canal contained 23 locks and gave the New York State canal system access to Lake Ontario at the city of Oswego.

Moving slowly through the city of Syracuse, we passed the Soldiers and Sailors Monument at Clinton Square, which was in plain sight from the canal boats. We could also see Onondaga Lake on our right. On our left passed the salt brine evaporation platforms, covering many acres; built close by the canal, they extended a mile or more along the south side of the stream. Syracuse was once this country's leading salt producer.

In this same area, traveling over the evaporators, was an overhead conveyor line, carrying soda ash from the south to the Solvay plant for processing. The conveyor consisted of trip buckets of from 300-500 pound capacity, spaced about one hundred feet apart. Suspended from a traveling endless cable, mounted on wooden poles fifteen feet high, the conveyor operated at a monotonous slow speed day and night. It extended alongside the canal for a mile or more.

Soon after leaving Syracuse we passed through Geres lock on the western edge of the city and then through a number of small familiar towns before we crossed the Seneca River on the second longest aqueduct on the Erie Canal.

The Seneca River area was also known as the most mosquito-ridden section along the canal, and we prepared for this part of the trip by assembling whatever mosquito repellents we had on hand.

The canal lock just west of Jordan was next, and I remember it well. Today, the village is one of the few towns that has kept the empty Erie Canal channel preserved within the town limits. The four-arched, 105-foot-long stone aqueduct is still in good condition, except for the removal of the wooden trunk that carried the canal over Skaneateles Creek. The empty channel has not been filled in, and is maintained in an attractive way with bright-colored flower beds in the summer time.

In this area, we travelled through some of the finest muck-lands in our state. The black rich muck gardens extended for miles along the canal, and many were operated by Italian families. Here some of the finest grade lettuce, celery, radishes, onions, and other garden produce were raised and marketed. When passing through here, Father was instructed by Mother to buy some of this fresh-grown produce. As the boats slowly passed by, the gardeners, who seemed to be on the look-out for customers, came up on the canal bank and asked if we needed any fresh vegetables. My father would ask the price of the produce in season and then put in an order for whatever he wanted that was for sale. The man or woman on the canalbank then walked into the gardens, picked what had been ordered and tossed the vegetables to Father on the slowly moving boats. The cost of the goods—a few coins—were inserted into a raw potato and tossed to the gardener on the canal bank. Both parties waved goodbye, quite satisfied with the transaction.

When passing by the muck gardens we were nearing the Montezuma area. Passing by here in later years, eastbound, with our boats loaded with gravel for Barge Canal construction, I was reminded of the stories told of digging through the muck along here, when the canal was built in Clinton's time.

As the loaded boats passed over this level, the slow movement of their passing stirred up the soft muck from the bottom of the canal. It gave the clear water the appearance of dark storm clouds moving in a blue sky. This thought came to me as I sat idly looking at the water from the stern rail of the hind boat as we traveled over this level between Jordan and Port Byron on a fine summer day.

The clear water came from three feeders flowing into the canal on the short summit-level between Geres Lock 50 and Lock 51 at Jordan. There were also three feeders flowing into the level between Jordan and Lock 52 at Port Byron. The source of the water of all the feeders came from the Finger Lakes and the surrounding area.

Weedsport was next, a small village along the canal. The name of the town always puzzled me: Why should a nice town be named for the lowly weed? My mind could not seem to connect the name with anything else. I eventually learned that it was first called Weeds Basin, named for two brothers. In 1821 Elihu Weed and Edward Weed, sons of Smith Weed, a wealthy Albany merchant, settled in what is now the village of Weedsport. They constructed or dug a basin on the south bank of the canal; this was a canal basin, a place where the canal had been widened out. Here the boats could be turned around, loaded and unloaded and not interfere with canal traffic. Today, an historical marker in Weedsport honors the Weed brothers.

Canal construction on this section of the canal had been finished by 1819, and in 1820 boats were running between Montezuma and Syracuse. By 1825 Weedsport was prosperous and large enough to arrange a celebration for the arrival of Governor Clinton and his company from the west. A brief account of an unfortunate incident that took place at Weedsport appears in the *Cayuga Republican,* published in Auburn on November 2, 1825: "Died at Weedsport on the morning of the 29th of last month, David Remington and Henry Whitman. They were killed by the accidental discharge of a 24 pounder, while they were acting as gunners at the canal celebration at that place. Remington was literally blown to atoms. Whitman survived about four hours. They were in the prime of life and both left young families to deplore their untimely exit."

Upon completion of the canal, Weedsport became the canal landing for Auburn, the seat of Cayuga County, which was about six miles south of the village. The town thrived on the merchandise shipped to and from Auburn via the canal until the railroads captured this business in the 1840s. The town slumped after losing Auburn's business, but gradually recovered, and today is a busy and thriving small town.

Three miles westward we passed through the village of Port Byron, a small quiet town that still had a canal drydock in operation. When possible, I was always on deck to see if any canal boats were in the drydock. Near the drydock a creek called the Owasco Outlet was spanned by a 98-foot-long aqueduct.

Drydocks were usually built near a stream lower than the canal; when emptying the drydock, the water drained by gravity through an opened valve into the stream. In the early days of the village, a water-powered mill erected on the Outlet speeded up the prosperity and building of the town.

First named Bucksville after two brothers who settled the town in 1798, the name was changed to Port Byron in 1825 when the canal was completed. Today, in front of a small house on a street corner in the village, a historical marker informs the reader that Henry Wells, founder of the Wells-Fargo Express Company, was a shoemaker and had lived in the house from 1827 to 1830. In 1868 the same Henry Wells founded Wells College, located in the heart of the Finger Lakes region at Aurora, New York.

Another historic marker in the village tells that Brigham Young, the Mormon Prophet, lived in a house 100 yards from the marker in 1831. He was baptized in 1832 at Mendon, New York.

A short distance west of the village, we passed through Lock 52 at Port Byron. The mention of this lock clearly recalls boyhood memories, as there was a grocery store at the lock and it was a convenient place to stock up on fresh food and boat supplies while locking through. When my folks bought a fair-sized order, this grocer also presented them with a bag of candy for us children. It usually consisted of peppermint sticks, licorice strings, horehound drops, gumdrops, eisenmoss, and chocolate drops. My brothers, sisters, and I eagerly looked forward to Port Byron lock when we passed up and down the canal and were always disappointed when we went through the lock late at night, for the store would be closed.

Just a few years ago, I learned of an event that took place at this lock in December of 1886. It was the winter the State lengthened Lock 52 on the heelpath side of the canal so that two boats could be locked through at the same time, without uncoupling. I heard of the story from Denny Pratt, who was born in 1878 and spent the first twelve years of his life on his parents' boat on the Erie Canal, boating lumber from the Tonawandas to Albany and New York City. One of his recollections was of a heart-breaking event that happened to his father, who had gone to Port Byron seeking work that winter on the lock-lengthening job. Work must have been scarce at the time, for there was a large crowd of men, many of them foreigners, looking for jobs at the worksite. A riot occurred when the hiring began, and Denny's father was stabbed. He never fully recovered from the wound and died the following August. Mrs. Pratt ran the boat until 1890 when she sold out. Denny said this ended his canal days at the age of twelve; but, except for the tragedy at Port Byron lock, he recalled a memorable and happy boyhood on the old Erie Canal.

The canal lock grocery store is long gone, but the Port Byron

Erie Canal Lock 52, built in 1851 is just west of the village of Port Byron, N.Y., and can be seen from the New York State Thruway. *Buffalo and Erie County Historical Society.*

lock, built in 1851 during the canal enlargement, sits high and dry in view of the New York State Thruway a short distance west of the village of Port Byron. To me, it stands there a silent reminder that it was once a part of the pathway of the busy and popular Erie Canal. The lock has been seen by an untold number of people traveling eastward on the Thruway.

Another thing that was unusual about Lock 52 was that when boaters were downbound on the Erie Canal, or traveling east from Buffalo, Port Byron lock was the first lock they encountered which locked the boats upward instead of down. Jordan lock was the same; the level between Jordan and Lock 50 was a short summit level. Locking down again at Geres Lock, boats locked up again through Locks 47-48 and 49 at Syracuse onto the summit or lower long level which stretched to Lock 46 at Utica. This and all of the forty-five locks between Utica and Albany locked downward.

Three miles or so west of Port Byron, we came to the quiet village of Montezuma. A historic marker in the village today notes that it was named for the Aztec emperor. Another marker tells that the Erie Canal was completed from here to Utica in 1819 and that the *Montezuma*, built here, was the first boat on the canal. The canal boat *Montezuma* carried passengers to Syracuse in 1820, five years before the official opening of the completed Erie.

This was the area that gave the first canal builders so much trouble. It was the swampiest, most fever-ridden section along the line of the canal. The soft muck and quicksand caused the canal banks to slide in as fast as they were dug. Also, many of the diggers died of fever before this section was finished.

Many improvements brought about by the digging of the canals in the area enabled the state to drain a vast acreage of swamps and turn it into rich farmland.

Montezuma is almost completely rural. The channels of the 1819 and the improved Erie Canal are within a few hundred feet of each other just west of the village, as is the Barge Canal at the northern edge of the town.

Nearly two miles after crossing the Seneca River on the long Montezuma aqueduct, we came to the small hamlet of Mays Point. Next was Clyde Lock and, then, the village of Clyde, which was well settled before the advent of the Erie Canal. The village no doubt took its name from the Clyde River, which was a highway for commerce until the canal was built.

A few miles farther on we came to Lock 54, which was called "Lock Berlin," a short distance south of the village of the same name. The canal banks along here were so overgrown with trees and plant life that nothing could be seen of the village whether we approached by day or night. It was one of the most lonesome and isolated spots along the entire canal.

A fleet of five Erie Canal boats being shoved by an Erie Canal steamer on the short Barge Canal level between Locks 2 and 3 of the Waterford flight of five locks. All six boats locked through at once. From Noble E. Whitford's *History of the Barge Canal.*

CHAPTER 9

Genesee Country
and the Upper Long Level

THREE MILES WEST of Lock Berlin, we passed through Lock 55 at Lyons, the seat of Wayne County. We were now entering the fruit belt of New York State.

A large vinegar works and apple processing plant was located here on the north side of the canal. In the fall, one could see car-loads of apples waiting on a railroad siding for processing in the plant. Soon after leaving the lock, we passed over a four-arched stone aqueduct, 130 feet long, built in 1841, spanning Mud Creek. Still there today at Lyons, on the western edge of the village, two of these old Erie Canal aqueduct piers can be seen, although the aqueduct has been destroyed.

A short distance east of the old aqueduct site, the Ganargua River (called Mud Creek on some maps) joins with the Canandaigua Outlet to form the Clyde River. A historic marker at Lyons tells us: "About 1795 near this spot the river view resembling that of Lyons, France, led Charles Williamson to rename the Forks Settlement, Lyons."

A mile or so further on, we came to Poorhouse Lock, located a short distance east of the Wayne County Poorhouse, from which the lock took its name. Built close to the lock was a red brick building that served as a store and as the locktender's living quarters. The old Poorhouse Lock 56 and the red brick building, now a private residence, are still there.

About two and a half hours later, still locking upward, we

The abandoned Erie Canal aqueduct which crossed Ganargua Creek at Lyons, N.Y. The picture, taken in the 1920s or 30s, shows the wooden trunk has been removed. Today only the shore-side piers of the aqueduct remain.

passed through the thriving village of Newark, once called Lockville because of the three locks built here, a short distance apart. At one time, a driver and a team of horses for hire was stationed there to assist canal fleets over the short levels between the three single locks. Four miles west of Newark we came to Port Gibson, which enjoys the distinction of being the only village in the small section of Ontario County that bordered on the Erie Canal. The village owes its existence to the construction of the canal, because the citizens were successful in having the county lines rearranged so that Ontario County had a port on the Grand Canal. The village was named for Henry B. Gibson, once a prominent banker in Canandaigua.

Palmyra was next. In the winter of 1788-89, John Swift and Col. John Jenkins purchased T12, R2, now Palmyra, and commenced the survey of the land into farm lots in March 1789. The town was thus well established before the Erie Canal was built. Here Joseph Smith resided as a young man and had his series of

The Erie Canal aqueduct crossing Mud Creek at Palmyra, N.Y. The stone mason's craft is displayed in this 90-foot-long aqueduct, which can still be seen today. Photo *circa* 1950. *Buffalo and Erie County Historical Society.*

famous visions that led to the founding of the Mormon Church. The nearby Ganargua Creek ran parallel with the canal in the Palmyra area. On the western outskirts of Palmyra, we would again cross Ganargua Creek on a 94-foot-long aqueduct. From here the creek goes in a southerly direction toward its source at Bristol Springs, near the south end of Canandaigua Lake.

A mile or so ahead was Macedon, an old canal town having two locks a short distance apart. The first and second (enlarged) Erie Canal channels are within a short distance from the Barge Canal in this area.

Moving on from Macedon, we came to Fairport, another

quiet village along the Erie, a pleasant town of shady streets and white painted houses. Near the towpath was a large vinegar works and apple processing plant. Fairport also had two large canning factories along the canal. Just about all the towns along the canal, between Clyde and Lockport, had some type of food-processing plant within their limits.

We traveled on toward Bushnell's Basin, another town named for an early settler. Through the years, a number of serious breaks occurred in the Erie Canal in the Bushnell's Basin area. The village was close to the place where a 60-foot high embankment carried the canal across the Irondequoit valley. A large culvert carried Irondequoit Creek under the canal at this location.

The distance from Fairport to Rochester by canal was seventeen miles; via highway, it was only seven miles. The part of the canal between Fairport, Bushnell's Basin, and Pittsford was known to canallers as the Oxbow Bend. The canal made what seemed like a half circle between the three towns. When slowly rounding the Oxbow in the evening, the circle of lights on top of the Cobbs Hill Reservoir in Rochester stayed in sight for hours.

Having passed around the big bend and then through Pittsford, we came to Brighton with its locks, on the eastern outskirts of Rochester. The four locks at Brighton and Rochester were the last ones we would pass through until we came to Lockport.

On leaving here we would be starting over the upper long level. This region would be a long, slow, hard pull for the mules for the next sixty miles. We would not hear the driver's hail of "Hooraw-lock" or pass through one for the next forty or fifty hours that it would take to cross this level with the partly loaded boats. Our only stop would be to change mules once every six hours. In addition, our progress would be painfully slow because of the current moving eastward on this upper long level.

The water, to supply and maintain the proper depth in the canal between Buffalo and Rochester, came from Lake Erie, a distance of eighty-six miles. Water supplied to the long level also generated electricity at Lockport; and it furnished water power for a few small mills along the canal before electric power became abundant. Some was used for irrigation; leaks and evaporation consumed more water. All of this contributed to the above-average current in the canal on the upper long level.

The original Erie Canal passed through the heart of the city of Rochester and was responsible for its early growth. It was a place of interest to any canaller, especially a young one. Here we crossed an aqueduct 802 feet 3 inches long, supported by seven arches high above the Genesee River. In the springtime one could look down and see the river's rushing waters tumbling through the gorge, providing power to the mills along its shores, while on the way to its outlet on Lake Ontario. At the eastern end of the aqueduct, there was the sharpest turn on the whole length of the canal, too sharp for the boats to be steered around in the regular way. Someone had to be on deck to assist the steersman around the sharp turn at the end of the aqueduct. The boats had to be partially uncoupled and then recoupled after making the turn.

Like most of the large cities along the canal, Rochester had a number of lift bridges. Long lines of traffic were held up on each side of the canal when the bridges were raised for our passage.

When the Erie Canal was first completed, the Rochester aqueduct was only wide enough for one-way boat passage. This caused many delays, fights, and arguments among the canal men. Completed in 1823, it contained nine Roman arches and leaked badly; it was replaced nineteen years later with a better aqueduct. This second one is still there; completed in 1842, it contained seven arches and did not leak. Being forty-five feet wide, it allowed boats to meet while crossing. Conforming to the new dimensions of the enlarged canal, it was built a little to the south of the first aqueduct. Both aqueducts were of the same basic construction— solid masonry.

A few miles beyond Rochester we crossed the Western Wide Waters, a sort of large basin in the canal about two hundred feet wide. In the fall, the previous year, on our way back to Tonawanda from Albany with the light or empty boats, we became windbound here for four hours. The wind was blowing strong, and as we crossed the wide waters with the wind hitting us broadside, we were blown against the towpath side of the canal. Trying with all their might, the mules were unable to move the boats; so there we stayed until the wind went down in the evening.

On this trip, however, the wide water was crossed without delay. Traveling over the 63-mile-long upper long level, we passed through some of the most beautiful countryside in New York

The old Erie Canal aqueduct crossing the Genesee River at Rochester, N.Y., as it looked in 1976. Built in 1842, it replaced one built in 1823 which leaked badly and only allowed the single passage of boats, thus causing delays, arguments, and fights. This aqueduct is 45 feet wide, and it allowed the double passage of boats. After the canal closed, Rochester built a subway in the canal bed. The aqueduct then carried subway trolleys across the river. Today an added upper level is used to carry vehicular traffic across the Genesee. *Buffalo and Erie County Historical Society.*

State, abounding in orchards, well-kept dairy farms, and fields of waving corn and grain. Much of this same sight can be viewed today.

As we moved westward from the Rochester and Genesee area,

we were about to pass through familiar towns and villages, most of which owed their founding to the Erie Canal. First was the small settlement of Greece, next was Adams Basin and Spencerport, then Brockport, a busy manufacturing town and the home of a State Teachers College since 1867. Holley was next, a small busy town named in honor of Myron Holley, who was one of the first Erie Canal Commissioners, active in the construction of the original Erie. The village owed its very existence to the canal.

Hulberton, a small village on the canal about midway between Holley and Albion, was the site of several sandstone quarries. One of these, the A. J. Squire Quarry, from which was obtained sandstone of a superior quality used principally for building purposes, provided stone for Buffalo's St. Paul's church, on Delaware Avenue, and for Sibley Hall at Rochester. Isaac Hulbert, for whom the village is named, was a native of Massachusetts who settled here in 1825, the year the Erie was completed. Three years later, about 1828, he built and opened the first grocery at this point on the canal. Another settler, George Squires, came from Columbia County, New York, also in 1825. He built the first frame building in the vicinity. Located near the north bank of the canal, it was later occupied by John Moore and Son as a canal grocery. This building is still standing, although it has been remodeled and occupied as a residence. Several abandoned water-filled sandstone quarries can still be seen in the Hulberton area.

Six miles farther on we came to a village that was named Newport when the Erie first opened. That village had become Albion, the seat of Orleans County, a pleasant town created by the Erie Canal. Between Albion and Medina are the small settlements of Eagle Harbor and Knowlesville. A mile or so before arriving at Medina, the canal crossed over Culvert Road, which passes under the canal through a tunnel or culvert. Before the Erie was enlarged, a viaduct crossed over the canal at this point. During the canal enlargement, the viaduct was replaced by a tunnel which was built in 1854. New York State lists the structure as Culvert #96. Built of Medina sandstone, the top of the curved ceiling is 13 feet above the single-lane roadway and has a vehicle clearance of 7½ feet; it is 15 feet wide at the bottom and 200 feet long. The southern end was lengthened to conform to Barge Canal width in 1910-11. It is still in use today—the only highway tunnel *under*

An early Erie Canal boat loading curb and building stone from the sandstone quarries near Albion, N.Y. Both derricks appear to be animal powered. Photo *circa* 1880. *Buffalo and Erie County Historical Society.*

the Erie Canal, a unique situation that Ripley once recorded in his "Believe It or Not" column. Culvert Road, which starts at Route 31, one mile east of Medina, is named for the structure under which it runs.

Approaching Medina from the west one time, I recall my father pointing out Ryan's abandoned quarry, the first one to be opened in this area by John Ryan. Quarrying Medina sandstone along the canal from Holly to Medina was a going industry from the time John Ryan opened the first quarry in the 1830s until concrete became popular in the early 1900s. Medina sandstone was used for paving, curb, and building stone; it was shipped to many distant localities. In 1908 my father's two boats carried rubble stone (chips or waste from cut stone) from Hulberton to Buffalo. This stone was used to fill and sink the wooden cribs which served as a foundation for extending the Buffalo breakwall.

Medina, a busy manufacturing town along the canal, had the only aqueduct between Rochester and Buffalo; it crosses Oak Orchard Creek, which has its outlet at Lake Ontario.

The next town was Middleport, so named because it was about halfway between Albion and Lockport. When nearing Middleport, we always looked forward to stopping at the canalside store of P. J. Fremoyle, where we would stock up on our supplies, mostly groceries, but sometimes shoes and clothing for the family. Fremoyle's was a well-stocked store that carried everything needed for the family, crew, mules, and canal boats. Mr. Fremoyle was a hearty, friendly man who did business longer than any canal store owner on the western end of the canal. He never failed to present Father with a bag of assorted candies for the children, always bid everyone a hearty goodbye, and he always told us to stop again when passing through.

We always stopped there whenever possible, because Father held off buying many of our supplies until we came to Middleport.

CHAPTER 10

Nearing the Journey's End

ABOUT FIVE MILES west of Middleport, we came to a landmark long familiar to boatmen. It was the Scheaffer Cold Storage Building, which was called the Fruit House or Cold Storage House by those who passed by it on the canal over a span of many years. Located one mile east of Gasport on the heelpath or south side of the canal, this building was unique in its day.

Built of Medina sandstone in 1870, with a white trimmed short square ornamental tower adorning its roof, the Scheaffer Building was primarily constructed for the storage of apples, and it stood there for nearly a century. It was of the same type built previously by the same family at Bristol in Bucks County, Pennsylvania. The walls were 27 inches thick, with an insulation space of 12 inches. It was cooled by ice until 1900, after which electric refrigeration was installed. The ice was on the second floor; a built-in drainage system carried the water from the melted ice out of the building. Being built alongside the canal, this took care of the drainage water and made it convenient for shipping the stored fruit by canal packet boats. The Scheaffer Cold Storage Building was destroyed by fire in 1967.

In a short time, we arrived at Gasport, which received its name from a scientific expedition traveling westward on the Erie Canal in 1826. Here they discovered a basin with a spring which emitted coal gas. A light applied to the bubbling gas produced a red flame. It was the expedition's recommendation that named the

The Scheaffer Cold Storage House on the canal near Gasport, N.Y., built in 1870 and destroyed by fire in 1967. Drawing by E. Mayes.

settlement Gasport. I had passed through Gasport many times before coming across this bit of history, and often wondered how this small village had come by its unusual name. Before the expedition's arrival, the town was named Jamesport.

The scientific expedition aboard the boat *Lafayette* that stopped at Gasport in 1826 was the forerunner of other specialized boats that would travel along the original Erie. Soon appeared "Gospel" or "mission" boats bringing religion to the people settled along its banks; "show boats" brought Shakespearean and other plays; and "circus boats" brought other entertainment. "Library boats," like the *Encyclopedia* of Albany, brought education, by way of books and lectures. Excursion boats took people on sightseeing trips and to places of entertainment along the canal. And, as mentioned earlier, there was also the bumboat that rowed out to passing canal boats to sell produce, foodstuffs, and notions.

Still there today is one set of the five combined locks of the Erie Canal at Lockport, N.Y. The diagonal grooves in the top of the iron railing, which separated the towpath from the locks, were made by the towlines as the mules pulled the boats upward through the locks. *Buffalo and Erie County Historical Society.*

The Grand Canal was a highway for many enterprises which soon appeared along its length.

A mile west of Gasport, we passed under a longer-than-usual highway bridge crossing the canal at Orangeport. This bridge was the settlement's only landmark along the canal. We were now nearing the end of our passage over the upper long level, five miles away at Lockport. With our partly loaded boats, it took us another four or five hours towing from Orangeport to Lockport.

When we arrived at the combines at Lockport, the lower lock was empty and the gates were open and ready for our first boat to enter. At Lockport there was a double set of five single locks. The northside set of locks were for upbound boats, and the other set was used for down boats. When locking down, the boats were flushed or swelled from lock to lock. When locking up, the mules towed the boats from lock to lock. An iron guard railing along the edge of the towpath kept the mules from accidentally falling into the locks.

Still there today are deep diagonal grooves worn in the top of the railing by the towline, as the mules pulled the boats up through the locks. Our upward passage was routine. We then went through the three-mile-long Rock Cut, which started at the head of the locks. It took three hours to tow through there. The current was strong in the narrow passage, and the mules labored hard to pull the boats against the current.

At Hitchings bridge, about a mile above the locks, we often stopped the boats and got a few pails of clear cold water that trickled from a spring in the rock wall above the towpath. The towpath, hewn from the side of the narrow cut, is still there to-day, and the spring still trickles, not far west of the Lockport locks. Just east of the spring is one of the escape holes cut into the rock wall of the canal down below the water's edge and used to re-trieve mules which might have accidentally fallen into the canal. (It is still there in the old towpath, but is now filled with con-crete.)

When the canal was first completed and opened above Lock-port, the towpath was on the edge of the Rock Cut, which in some sections was thirty feet deep. Later, this dangerous condition was improved by lowering the towpath in the cut to six or seven feet above the water level.

Two miles after we left the Rock Cut behind, we cautiously passed through one of the twin stone guard locks located five miles west of Lockport. Another two miles farther on we came to Pendleton and started over the eleven-mile canalized section of Tonawanda Creek. This was the most crooked part of the old Erie between Albany and Buffalo, and the only natural stream used as a part of the enlarged Erie Canal.

Just before we came to Pendleton, our team crossed a tow-

A pair of animal-towed Erie Canal boats moving westward in the three-mile-long rock cut above Lockport, N.Y. Photo *circa* early 1900s.

path change bridge. From here, the towpath followed the south side of the canal to the western outskirts of Tonawanda. On entering Tonawanda Creek, a long two-span wooden bridge carried the mules over the creek entrance to the part used as the canal. As the current was easier here, it would take about nine more hours to finish our upbound trip with the two partly loaded boats. We had left Lockport at dusk and would arrive at Tonawanda the next morning.

After climbing into my bunk in the after boat cabin that evening, I lay awake for a while, with the anticipation of our arrival home once again, and thinking of visiting my boyhood hangouts and seeing my friends and schoolmates. I fell asleep while listening to the soft murmur of the current and eddies of the water as it swirled around the stern of the boat, as we slowly moved toward Tonawanda.

To some, it may not have been a very attractive small city, with its numerous bridges crossing the canal or creek to North Tonawanda; the old battered wooden dam across the creek just

Junction of the Erie Canal and Tonawanda Creek at Pendleton, N.Y. The three-span bridge in the foreground carried the towpath across Tonawanda Creek, which branches off to the right. The first bridge in the background changes the towpath to the north side of the canal. A highway bridge crosses just past the change bridge. Photo *circa* early 1900s. *Buffalo and Erie County Historical Society.*

east of the railroad bridge; the old wooden Long Dock supported on wooden piles, which ran from the Delaware Street bridge, westward to the Tonawanda end of the old Dam; the trains running at street level through the heart of both cities; the bridges crossing Ellicott Creek; more bridges in the business district, crossing the canal from North to South Niagara Street; the old lock and lock bridge on North Niagara Street; the lumber piled on the docks along the river up past Gibson Street, blotting out the scenic view of the Niagara; and the lumber yards, box shops, and planing mills, the bumpy brick-paved main streets, and at this time, many that were dusty, muddy, and still unpaved.

To me, Tonawanda was a familiar and welcome sight. It was

Water sports on the Erie Canal, between North and South Niagara Streets at Tonawanda, N Y., on July 4, 1910. Note greasy pole extending out over the canal in background.

home. I was on the lookout for it an hour or two before we arrived, asking Father how far away it was, and how long it would take to get there.

Arriving at Tonawanda, we put the mules in the bowstable. A tug then towed our boats a half mile up Ellicott Creek to their destination at the Roofing Company. Fourteen days had elapsed since we had loaded the fine white gravel at Oyster Bay, Long Island.

Tomorrow would be a busy day for Father. He would supervise the unloading of the boats. He would also find time to collect the balance of his freight money and contact a lumber broker for return loads down the canal.

CHAPTER 11

The Greatest Lumber Port in the World

T HE TONAWANDAS' importance as a lumber center began building up soon after the Civil War, and in 1867 the first cargo
for distribution to other cities or towns was received. The location
on the Niagara River at the end of the upper Great Lakes and its
position near the western end of the Erie Canal made it an ideal
location for receiving and shipping lumber from upper lake ports.

In 1888 there were six miles of lumber docking covering the
area on the waterfront, four miles in North Tonawanda, and two
miles in Tonawanda.

The 1884 season was the peak year for shipments of lumber
departed from the Tonawandas via the Erie Canal. A canal boat
at that time averaged 180,000 to 200,000 board feet per load. So
the above figure was the equivalent of 2,023 boat loads.

Although canal shipments lessened each year after 1884,
lumber received from the upper lake ports increased every year
until 1890, when 718,650,900 board feet arrived in the Tonawandas. That year saw the Tonawandas become the greatest lumber port in the world, outranking Chicago receipts by millions of
board feet. Each year after 1890 saw lumber shipments to the
Tonawandas dwindle as the forest area in the northwest was
cleared. Canal shipments of lumber from the Tonawandas ceased
a few years after the closing of the Erie Canal.

Some sixty-three lumber companies operated over the years
in the Tonawandas. Many of the companies operated what were

Partly loaded pair of westbound animal-towed Erie Canal boats passing the lumber docks on the outskirts of Tonawanda. The Niagara River is in the background. Photo *circa* 1890. *Courtesy of Historical Society of the Tonawandas.*

called "box shops," which manufactured wooden boxes and crates of all sizes, for the packing and shipping of all types of merchandise. The box shops began closing in the late 1920s as the cheaper corrugated paper cartons gained popularity. There were also sawmills turning out lath and shingles, railroad ties, also planing mills that turned out moldings and finished lumber, doors, window sashes and other finished products. Other companies simply shipped or forwarded the rough lumber to distant places by railroad and canal.

Many of the local lumber companies owned and operated their own lake vessels, which brought the rough lumber to the Tonawandas.

The locally owned wooden vessels usually wintered here, and each spring the smell of pitch and oakum scented the air, along with the sound or ring of caulking mallets that could be heard

An early wooden lumber steamer unloading railroad ties at Tonawanda, N.Y.
The leather aprons on lumber handlers were used to protect clothing and to
help slide the lumber across the men's knees. Each man furnished his own
apron. Photo *circa* 1890s. *Buffalo and Erie County Historical Society.*

along the waterfront as the vessels were being readied for the sea-
sonal lumber trade. The winter of 1917-18 saw the Tonawandas
still harboring eight lumber steamers or "hookers," as they came
to be called, and thirteen of their tow barges, making a total of
twenty-one lake lumber vessels in the Tonawandas that winter.
The following winter of 1918-19 saw eleven steamers and ten tow
barges in layup at the Tonawandas. The winter layup fleets gradually dwindled away, along with the lumber shipments that were
once received in the Tonawandas.

While the Tonawandas were achieving the title of "The Greatest Lumber Port in the World," the influx of lake sailors and canallers spawned a red light district in Tonawanda that was known all
over the Great Lakes and the length of the Erie Canal.

The district was known as Goose Island and the name went back to the early days of Tonawanda. Large flocks of geese made this section along the Niagara River front, of what was then the village of Tonawanda, a stopover during the migration season.

It seemed that whenever I met a sailor or a canaller, when I was away from home, after they found out where I was from, they always asked: "How is everything on Goose Island?" I seem to recall that they always had a look of relief on their faces when I said all right. Even though it was raided now and then by the law authorities, this section of Tonawanda remained in existence until some time in the 1930s when it was closed for good.

In the early 1900s, I often heard my father and other boatmen discuss a riot which had taken place in 1895 at Scribner's lumber docks in Tonawanda. The Scribner office was located near the river about where the City Hall now stands on North Niagara Street. At that time, the company's lumber docks extended along the river from their office up past the old canal spillway to about Franklin Street. Prior to the riot a Boatmen's Association had been organized for the boatmen's protection against what they considered unfair practices and for the purpose of maintaining fair and profitable lumber freight rates on the canal. One of the unfair practices complained about by the boatmen was the fact that some boats would arrive and lay in Tonawanda for a week or more waiting for loads. Others, on their arrival, would load ahead of those that had been waiting. This was the cause of much dissent and was probably a contributing factor to the riot.

At the time of the riot, the members of the Association were on strike against the lumber shippers, and refused to load because the freight rates offered were so low they could hardly make expenses.

While the strike was going on, a Captain Phillips and his son, who owned and operated two lumber boats, arrived in Tonawanda. They were told about the strike and requested not to load until the freight rates were raised to a profitable level. They could not be dissuaded, claiming their financial plight made it imperative for them to load even for a small profit. Against the objections of the Association, their boats were towed to Scribner's lumber docks and were to be loaded the next day.

As a result of this decision, ugly feelings amongst the boatmen were running high against the Phillipses. That evening many of the boatmen were drinking in the saloons about town. Near midnight a crowd of boatmen gathered in town and marched to the lumber docks, determined to prevent the Phillipses from loading their boats.

Captain Phillips and his son refused to listen. During the argument, the Phillipses had remained aboard the boats and the crowd which stayed on shore suddenly turned into an angry mob. One of them threw a brick which struck the younger Phillips in the head, killing him instantly. A revolver shot, fired by someone in the mob, killed Captain Phillips. The mob then cut the boats loose, allowing them to drift down the river, crossways against the Tonawanda Island swing bridge, held there by the current, with the dead men aboard. The two boats were found the next morning and towed back to Tonawanda. What a terrifying time it must have been for Flora Phillips, who had remained in the cabin all night.

Many members of the mob were served warrants. It was said that the streets of the village were like those of a ghost town when the papers were served on the men who were arrested. After a long drawn-out trial, only two persons served time in prison for the crime committed against the Phillipses.

A boatman named George Hyde was one of the men sent to prison. I gathered from hearing my father talk to other boatmen who knew Mr. Hyde that none of them thought him guilty of the crime for which he was convicted. It was believed he had been made a scapegoat for someone else, although he was one of the mob. Some time after he was released from Auburn prison, I was introduced to Mr. Hyde by my father. He was on a canal boat at Port Byron. Then elderly and white-headed, he did not look like a man who would take part in a mob action or be guilty of the crime for which he had been sent to prison.

Sometime in the early 1920s, I saw the long-vacant office building of the Scribner Lumber Company being loaded on two canal boats, lashed side by side. It was being moved across the Erie Canal to a site on South Niagara Street, where it was remodeled and is still used as a residence.

Some time ago, I ran across a shipping bill made out to the owner of two canal boats. The bill was dated October 18, 1906, and was made out to Mrs. Fred Broadbeck, Master of the canal boat, *David Charley,* having aboard 185,000 board feet of white pine lumber, consigned to Arnold & Co., Albany. The freight rate was $2.10 per M., and $150 was advanced to the owner or master for the express purpose of defraying expenses en route to Albany, the balance to be paid on delivery.

In those days the average time required for a pair of animal-towed boats to reach Albany from Tonawanda required eight days. Allowing three days to unload two boats, and seven days to return light or empty to Tonawanda, the average time required for a round trip was twenty-one days.

Mrs. Broadbeck was a widow whose husband had left her the two boats which she and her son-in-law operated for a number of years carrying lumber between Tonawanda and Albany. Born in Kentucky, she was a family friend. On retiring from the canal, she lived out her retirement in Tonawanda. She is the same person who was interviewed by the author of *Body, Boots & Britches.*

Old records show that the first work done on the western end of the first Erie Canal was the construction of a dam across Tonawanda Creek at Tonawanda in the spring of 1823. The dam raised the level of the creek four or four and a half feet above normal. As a result, no locks were necessary between Buffalo and Lockport. The canal sloped one inch per mile between these places and provided a continuous supply of water from Lake Erie to the Brighton Locks on the eastern edge of Rochester.

Although the dam helped to solve a vital water supply problem for the canal, it created another in the Tonawandas area, that of flooding in the villages and the surrounding countryside, especially in the springtime.

As a result of many lawsuits against the State, because of the flooding, the State, then with Canal Funds, built what were called State Ditches to ease the flooding. The ditches began in the low areas and emptied into the Niagara River, in both North Tonawanda and Tonawanda, but had little effect in solving the flooding.

The dam was lowered two feet in 1871. This must have eliminated the flooding in North Tonawanda, as that State Ditch served no purpose thereafter, but spring flooding remained a problem in Tonawanda until the dam was removed.

The old dam was built with a canal lock at its north end, for locking boats to and from the Niagara River. The first lock also handled the lockage of many rafts of logs and timber that were shipped on the first Erie Canal.

In later years the location of the lock was changed. In 1874 a single enlarged sidecut lock was built in the heart of the Tonawanda business district. Through this old lock, over the years, many canal boats carrying millions of board feet of lumber passed from the Niagara River into the canal. The boats delivered the lumber to all the cities along the Erie Canal and along the Hudson River. But it was the Albany Lumber District at the eastern end of the canal that received the bulk of the shipments from the Tonawandas.

As far as I know, the old Tonawanda sidecut lock is still in good condition, now buried by a land fill, when the Erie Canal was filled in during the 1930s. Although it was said to be deeper and wider than any other section, the nine-mile stretch of canal between Tonawanda and Black Rock had the strongest current of any part of the canal. Loaded boats bound for Buffalo, stopped at Tonawanda, ran out the other team on the towpath and used six mules to make headway against the stronger current.

Of the twelve towpath change bridges on the Erie Canal, four of them were at the western end. One at Pendleton changed the towpath from the north to the south side of the canal. A mile above the Tonawanda business district it changed back to the north side; at Black Rock, it again changed back to the south side. At Jersey Street in Buffalo, it again changed to the other side. In Buffalo, very little evidence of the canal is left. The Niagara section of the New York State Thruway covers the route of the old canal from Black Rock to where it terminated at the harbor.

Erie Canal sidecut lock to the Niagara River, Tonawanda, N.Y. Eastern Lumber Company's "lighters" are locking through to take on lumber from lake vessel in background. When loaded, they were locked back into the canal and unloaded at the company's dock on Ellicott Creek which adjoined the canal a short distance from the lock. Note canal boat center-board leaning against fence. The weather tower at right displayed signal lamps or pennants to convey weather information to lake-bound mariners. Photo 1912.

CHAPTER 12

From Lumber to Gravel Boating

B EFORE THE TRIP to New York City, described in detail in the preceding several chapters, the lumber business began to taper off, a situation which was of considerable concern to canal men like my father.

The year 1909 had been a slow season for lumber shipments. On our first trip we carried two boatloads of white pine which we unloaded at one of the yards in the Albany lumber district. We returned to Tonawanda light; and, after a lengthy wait, we took aboard two more loads of white pine—this time for Syracuse. On that trip, Father had to arrange for the unloading of the boats. I recall that he had a hard time hiring men to help with the unloading. The work was temporary and very arduous, and he could hire only a few transients or hobos who would work just long enough to earn a few dollars for drinking money. The two drivers had been paid off; so, Father and the wheelsman worked with the few lumber handlers that could be hired. My brother Jim and I were too young to handle lumber, and we whiled away the time at a nearby sandpile. I'll never forget the beating we took from two older boys who jumped us while we were playing there one afternoon; yet, even though we went back to the boats blubbering, we returned to the sandpile the next day.

We were a week unloading at Syracuse on that trip, and afterwards we headed back to Tonawanda with light boats instead of cargo.

The lumber shipping situation had not improved, but Father was able to secure two loads of pig iron for delivery at Bayonne, New Jersey, as well as two scotch steamship boilers destined for New York City. The second boat was partly loaded with pig iron, and the two boilers, weighing about 15 tons each, were set on blocking built up from the bottom of the boat. They were too large in diameter to be lowered all the way down into the cargo hold. After the boilers were stowed, sufficient pig iron was loaded to bring the boats to a 6-foot draft and thus give the boilers enough head room to clear the bridges along the canal.

We had no trouble with bridges until we left the lock at Frankfort. To start the boats out of the lock, the locktender gave us such a large swell that it raised the boats high enough to carry away the wooden footbridge crossing the lower end of the lock. This meant a delay below the lock for some time until the canal authorities were contacted. Meanwhile, the footbridge remained perfectly balanced on top of the boiler on our boat.

It was decided that we should proceed and stop under the next highway bridge crossing the canal, where the footbridge would be lifted clear of the boiler. This plan worked well, and we went on our way leaving the unwanted burden hanging on the bridge, close to the heelpath side of the canal a short distance below the Frankfort lock. All of us were relieved to be rid of the odd-looking contraption perched on top of our unusual cargo.

Although there were no further incidents with the boilers, I recall that it was very hot on that midsummer trip. To get some relief from the heat in the cabins, my uncle got the idea of placing some mattresses and bedding in the boiler fireboxes. It was a shady spot and a breeze circulated through our makeshift sleeping quarters. We enjoyed some comfortable naps and slept soundly on hot nights for the balance of the trip. All too soon we delivered the boilers to New York City and unloaded the pig iron in Bayonne. The return trip to Tonawanda was made, unfortunately, without a cargo.

Lumber shipping continued to fall off, and we finished up the season making only two more trips to Albany with white pine.

Early in the spring of 1910, Father received word that there would be four or five good seasons ahead for boatmen who would convert their boats for the hauling of stone and gravel. There was need for a number of Erie canal boats to haul the thousands of cubic yards of gravel required to build the rest of the locks, concrete docks, retaining walls, bridge abutments, and culverts that were still to be constructed in many places along the Barge Canal route. Many cubic yards of rubble stone also had to be hauled for rip-rapping the new canal banks.

On receiving this information, my father and other canal boatmen had suitable decks installed for carrying stone and gravel. These "false decks" or "stone decks" decreased the depth of a boat's cargo hold by three feet. They made the boat stronger and more efficient for carrying, loading, and unloading the much heavier cargo. After the new false decks were installed, Father remarked that he wished the boats had had them in 1908, as he had spent part of that season hauling rubble stone from Hulberton to Buffalo to serve as a base for Donnelley's Breakwall, located near the entrance to Buffalo harbor, to give the Black Rock channel and the Barge Canal terminal greater protection in rough weather.

Our mules were sold: the boats now would be towed by a tug. Most of the cargoes would be handled by steam-powered derricks equipped with clam shells (buckets).

In 1910, we began boating gravel to construction sites along the upper long level between Lockport and Rochester. The gravel that was loaded on our boats at North Tonawanda had been pumped or dredged from the Niagara River.

That summer, while waiting to unload gravel at Spencerport for the Barge Canal retaining wall being built in that village, I fell into the canal for the second time. Our loaded boats had been tied up for the night in the village, along the sloping bank of the old canal, where they would start to unload the next day. That morning, Mother and I got up and dressed about the same time. She put the coffee pot on the wood-burning stove. The fire had already been started by Father who had gotten up earlier. Needing potatoes to cook for breakfast, Mother decided to take me on deck with her, as the rest of the children were still sleeping. Father was busy pumping out the head boat with the tin hand pump as we came on deck.

Because of the sloping canal bank, the boats were about six feet out from the shore. A plank from the boats to the canal bank was used for getting on and off of the boats. While Mother was busy getting the potatoes out of the deck box, I went out on the middle of the springy plank and began bouncing up and down. When she noticed me, she frantically called to me to stop jumping and come back on the boat. I just kept on until I missed my footing and fell smack into the canal. Mother immediately called to my father, who came running back, jumped in, and got me out of the canal again. This time I was a little older, and was able to splash about and keep my head above water. I was only a few feet from the canal bank, but I would not have made it alone.

The next season we were still boating gravel on the upper long level and carrying gravel for Barge Canal construction work at Middleport. One time, as we waited for the boats to unload, my brother Jim and I went over to the drydock to watch the activity going on. Tied up in the canal near where we were standing was a work raft. One of the workmen had come to move it across the front of the drydock, and, at our request, he gave us a ride. All went well until we reached the other side. My attention was elsewhere as we unexpectedly bumped the dock. I lost my balance and fell in the canal. Another dunking! This time, when I came to the surface, the raftsman grabbed me by the hair and pulled me out of the water.

I cannot remember being very much frightened each time I was saved from drowning. Maybe it was because each time I fell in, someone was nearby to get me out quickly. I once fell from a lumber dock into the Niagara River and got out by myself. That time I *was* really frightened because there was no one in sight.

Some of the construction sites we hauled gravel to, in this section for the Barge Canal, required only from two to six boat loads of gravel. This amount was sufficient for a pair of bridge abutments, a short retaining wall or a large culvert, such as the one we hauled gravel for at Eagle Harbor, where a good-sized creek passes under the Barge Canal. This construction site required only a few boatloads of gravel. The contractor did not go to the expense of transporting and setting up a steam-powered, stiff-legged wooden derrick to clam the gravel out of the boats. He had them unloaded entirely by manpower.

The boats were tied up against the sloping canal bank, with heavy wooden planks laid across the open water between the shore and the boat. Connecting planks in line with the shore planks were laid across the boats amidship, at the cargo hold. Six men with wooden wheelbarrows wheeled the gravel ashore as fast as men with hand shovels loaded the barrows. A day's work then was ten or twelve hours. The average Erie Canal boat carried 150 to 160 cubic yards of gravel, and it required eighteen men to unload a boat in one day. In comparison, a steam derrick equipped with a clam shell could unload two boats in one day.

The laborers who unloaded the boats were mostly Italians who worked up a healthy appetite by lunch time. At noon their lunch consisted of a loaf of flat, round Italian bread, sliced through the middle, filled with fried or scrambled eggs, and sausage or cheese. Being accustomed to ordinary sandwiches, I was amazed at this type of lunch.

At no time during the reconstruction or conversion of the Erie Canal to the Barge Canal, between Tonawanda and the town of Greece on the upper long level, was the flow of canal traffic halted. There were some delays due to congestion at Lockport, because one flight of the five twin locks were removed to make way for the construction of the two-flight Barge Canal locks, which took two or more years to complete. During their construction, both upbound and downbound boats had to use the one set of locks.

At the end of 1911, the hauling of Niagara River gravel for the work on the upper long level was nearly finished. Barge Canal construction in this area was nearing completion. That winter, our boats were put under contract to haul gravel for the Barge Canal construction for the part of the canal to be built through the central part of the State.

The gravel for the work on this part of the canal came from a huge pit close to the Erie Canal about two miles east of the village of Palmyra. The deposit covered a large area; it furnished the gravel used for the section between Rochester and Rome, also for the Cayuga-Seneca Canal, as far as Geneva.

Here at the gravel pit, alongside the canal, a large wooden hopper-type storage bin had been erected, capable of holding about four boatloads of gravel. Each boatload averaged 150 cubic yards. The boats would be tied up alongside the hoppers; the chutes were then lowered over the boat, and gravel would flow by gravity into the hold. Four to six boats could be loaded in one day when everything went smoothly.

A narrow-gauge railway was used to haul the material. A steam shovel loaded small side-dumping rail cars, hauled by a steam dinky engine which shuttled back and forth from the gravel pit to the canalside loading dock. Here the gravel was dumped into a small pit and carried up to the top of the storage bins by an endless belt. Another belt distributed the material into separate bins.

Starting in 1912, the years we spent boating gravel from Palmyra were enjoyable ones for me and Jim. As soon as the boats arrived in Palmyra, we would go off roaming the countryside, or fishing from an old rowboat adrift in the canal. Tiring of this, we would just watch the activity around the gravel pit loading dock, occasionally asking the engineer on the dinky engine to let us ride on the engine for a few trips. We also liked to climb to the top of the gravel-hopper and watch the boat-loading operations.

We sometimes walked into town to get rid of our pocket money or to run a small errand for Mother. On the way back, we might stop to see Mr. and Mrs. Oaks, who operated a farm about a half mile from the gravel pit. They were fine people with a well-kept farm. The two families became well acquainted, and Mother and we children sometimes visited with the Oakses while waiting for the boats to load. It was there I learned something of farm life, watching the milking of the cows, separating the cream, churning the butter, caring for the livestock, and seeing the many other chores and duties that had to be done to operate a farm.

Clear, cool spring water ran from a one-inch pipe driven into the hillside near the loading dock at Palmyra. It spilled over the edge of a sawed-off wooden tub placed under the pipe, draining away into the canal. The spring flowed constantly, night and day; and we never failed to fill the boats' drinking water barrels at this spring. I never tasted water that could equal it anywhere. It was cold on the hottest summer days.

On a few occasions, when we arrived at the gravel pit to load, a major breakdown in the loading mechanism would cause a delay for a couple of days or more. When this happened, three or four fleets of boats would collect there waiting to load. The boatmen, many of them old friends, made the best of the interruption of their daily routine by visiting back and forth. A few of them went into town, to take care of any business matters they might have, and then stop in a local tavern and "bend the elbow," not too wisely, but very well. They returned to the boats in the late after-noon in a jovial mood; feeling good, they frequently slipped their young sons some change. After supper, a half dozen of us, who were all from boating families, walked into town on a warm sum-mer evening and went to the show—silent movies in those days.

Walking back to the boats one evening along Main Street in Palmyra, we approached a pool room in front of which a group of men and a few boys were standing. As we passed by, one of the oldest boys stepped out and began pushing and shoving the oldest lad in our crowd, challenging him to fight.

Our friend, Hy, was a good-natured, easy-going lad, but he could not avoid the challenge. Squaring off, the two started slug-ging it out on the sidewalk in front of the pool hall. In a short time, the challenger, who was taking some mean shots to the head and getting the worst of it, began hollering quits. When the fight was over, while Hy was putting on his jacket, one of the town sports who had been a bystander, walked up to Hy and gave him a dollar. The loser and instigator of the fight wanted part of the prize money, but got nothing. The rest of the way back to the boats we were all keyed up over what had happened, and very much elated that Hy had won the fight.

In 1912 six or eight fleets of boats were hauling gravel from Palmyra. All of the fleets were towed by canal tugs, except one. This fleet was still towing with its own mules. The two boats were owned and operated by an old gentleman with a snow-white beard. He was from Auburn, New York, and was most religious. All of the canal fleets operated day and night seven days a week, except the boats of the old gent from Auburn. He would tie his boats up before midnight on Saturday and start out again after midnight on Sunday. He had owned and operated boats on the canal for many years in this same manner and always went to church on Sunday wherever they were tied up.

Another fleet of boats well known at Palmyra was owned and operated by a man with a wife and a large brood of children. The scruffy appearance of this family was the cause of much un-favorable comment from other canal families. They were known as "the dirty dozen," because of their aversion to combs, soap, and water.

Our two boats, and the two boats of another family, also

from Tonawanda, were towed by a small wooden tug capable of operating in the old canal for the four seasons we boated gravel from Palmyra. We ran twenty-four hours a day when towing through the canal. The tug crew consisted of five men: a captain and a mate, two engineers, and a cook. The captain, the mate, and the two engineers worked six hours on and six hours off. The engineers operated the engine and also fired the coal-buring boiler. The male cook prepared the meals, washed the dishes, and kept the galley clean and supplied with food. He also filled in as a deckhand, day or night, when needed topside.

I had more than one bowl of turtle chowder, prepared by the cook on that tug. There were a lot of snapping turtles in the canal between Palmyra and Grove Springs, and the fishing was excellent between Palmyra and Syracuse. Aboard the tug, the crew had a bamboo pole with a sharp hook attached to one end. When a turtle was sighted swimming in the canal, the tug would be steered along side of the snapper. A man on deck would hook the turtle under its shell and haul it aboard the tug. They would, on occasion, catch some hapless farmer's duck swimming in the canal, by the same method.

The first year at Palmyra, we boated gravel for the Barge Canal Locks 32 and 33, which were located between Pittsford and the Genesee River. Gravel hauling to these locks was delayed for five weeks that season, because of a break or washout in the canal at Bushnell's Basin. While the break was being repaired, we hauled gravel for the Palmyra Lock 29 and Macedon Lock 30, which was a short haul of two and three miles from the gravel pit.

The break at Bushnell's Basin, which occurred on the morning of September 3, 1912, washed out a 500-foot section of the north bank of the canal. The break happened at the height of the grain shipping season. Temporary repairs were rushed through by emergency crews working night and day. The mule teams of many of the delayed canal boats were put to work hauling dirt to build up the embankment. Then a temporary wooden flume, or trough, was constructed to carry the boats over the break until a permanent channel could be built.

The flume was just 22 feet wide, allowing only a single passage of boats. This reduced the width of the canal by two thirds, and caused too fast a current in the flume for the boats to be hauled through by animal power or the low-powered steam canal fleets and the small steam tugs of that day. A steam dummy engine was installed at the western or upper end of the flume, and westbound boats were pulled slowly through by a long steel cable attached to the drums of the engine.

The cable was also attached to the eastbound boats, so that they could be eased slowly through without attaining too great a speed from the fast current and cause damage. The flume remained in use until permanent repairs were made that winter. At the cost of $75,000, shipping was under way again five weeks after the break occurred.

This section of the canal was also the scene of earlier breaks. On May 20, 1911, for instance, newspapers reported a mammoth break in the canal between Pittsford and Bushnell's Basin that would take several weeks to repair. "Tore hole in bank one hundred fifty feet wide. Canal emptied between Pittsford and Clyde," one report read.

The soil in the area of this high embankment at Bushnell's Basin consisted mostly of sand and gravel; any small seepage would soon cut a hole through the soft soil and, in a short time, rupture the canal bank. It was a rather important area in its own right, because some of the gravel for Barge Canal construction work was boated from Bushnell's Basin.

After the flume was in operation following the September 1912 break, we again began delivering gravel to Locks 32 and 33. When we arrived at the flume with the loaded boats on our way west, the tug let go of the boats and crossed the flume by itself. The cable was then attached to our boats and we were pulled slowly across by the steam dummy. Looking down into the Irondequoit Valley while crossing the flume, I could see the wreckage of a canal boat that had been carried through the embankment in an earlier washout.

Despite such delays and difficulties, we finished our trips to Locks 32 and 33 before the season ended, and we next began delivering gravel to Newark for the construction of Barge Canal Lock 28. This lock would replace the three older Erie Canal locks then in use in the village. Gravel was also required for concrete bridge abutments for three bridges, a canal terminal, and long retaining walls along the canal in the village. We also delivered gravel to Lock 28A, "Poorhouse Lock," which I mentioned first in Chapter 9. The home from which the lock took its name was a short distance from the lock, set back a short way from the south side of the canal.

While we were unloading at Poorhouse Lock, we visited with my father's brother, my Uncle John Garrity, who had retired from the canal and was operating a canalside farm, near where our boats were tied up. He had a red brick farmhouse surrounded by a picket fence, and while playing there with my brothers, one of them stretched a string across the gate post. I came running pell mell out of the yard, and stumbled because of the string, and my kneecap struck the corner of a stepping stone used for people alighting from horsedrawn buggies, cutting a large gash in my knee. I recall this mishap very well, and I still have the scar to refresh my memory.

We finished the season of 1912 hauling gravel to Poorhouse Lock. It had been a busy and active season for everyone. On our way back home, the tug and the four boats stopped at the gravel pit in Palmyra, where we picked up some winter supplies that were ready for us at the nearby Oaks Farm. My parents purchased three barrels of assorted apples (which I recall cost just $2 a *barrel*), twenty bushels of potatoes, thirty heads of cabbage, two bushels of squash, a bushel of beets, a bushel of carrots, and a tub of butter. All of this produce was stored in the dirt-floored, unheated cellar of our home in Tonawanda. It would all be used up before spring came around. Boatmen were never sure of working in the winter, and many of them stocked up at low prices from canalside farms and stores at the end of each season.

A very harrowing experience for my mother happened that fall soon after our return to Tonawanda. When we arrived there that morning, I had jumped off of the boats as soon as they were tied up. The tug then went on to its winter quarters in Buffalo, and I looked up some of my friends, staying until lunch time, when I returned to the boats to eat. It was then I learned that a lot of excitement had been caused by my five-year-old brother, Charles, while I was off saying hello to my friends.

When we first arrived in Tonawanda, the boats had been tied up near the old canal lock to remove some gear and supplies Father had brought home for one of his friends. After taking care of the chore, it was decided to move the boats by hand, one at a time, and tie them up in front of our house, which faced the canal at 78 N. Niagara Street, where we could unload the winter supplies he had brought home, and also have the boats handy to look after during the winter. While he and the steersman were busy pulling the second boat against the current under the Seymour Street bridge, Charles and my younger sister Gladys were sitting on top of the cabin, where my mother had placed them, with strict instructions not to get down, never dreaming of what would happen.

Glad to be home again, they were viewing the familiar scenes and activities along the street on each side of them, as the boat moved slowly up the canal. Suddenly, with Mother busy in the cabin, my small sister excitedly called down, "Mommy, Mommy, Charles is hanging on the bridge!" By the time Mother realized what had happened and rushed up out of the cabin, the boats had moved a considerable distance, and Charles was left hanging to the underside of the bridge over open water. Father was quickly told of his young son's plight. Stopping the slowly moving boat as soon as he could, he started moving back under the bridge, never thinking he would make it before Charles would have to let go. In the meantime, a considerable crowd had collected along the towpath, many of them shouting encouragement to the young lad to hold on just a little longer. An acquaintance of ours had his coat and shoes off, ready to dive in if the boy should let go. But Charles surprised everyone: he hung on until the boat was moved back under him and willing arms lifted him back on the boat. A sigh of relief came from the people on the towpath and many shouted congratulations because he had hung on so long. He must have hung on that bridge for ten minutes!

I thought Charles must have gotten the idea of hanging onto the bridge from me and my older brother, Jim, because it was a stunt we sometimes pulled as our boats were being towed through the canal when the boats were empty. We would stand on the bow of the boat and catch hold of the underside of a bridge and hold on while the empty midship passed under us and then let go when the stern of the boat came under us, and drop back on deck. But my little five-year-old brother said that as the cabin had passed part way under the bridge, he had stood up and put his hands on the bridge and started pushing to help move the boat along; then, before he was aware of it, the boat had passed from under him and he was still hanging onto the bridge.

At any rate, this personal family incident brought a memorable end to the first season of hauling from the Palmyra gravel pit. Father anticipated a few more seasons at least, and, with the increased construction for the new Barge Canal waterway, I expected to see some changes taking place along the route of the old Erie.

CHAPTER 13

Hauling Gravel from Palmyra

THE NEXT SPRING, in 1913, when we came back to the gravel pit, changes were already in evidence in the canal in this locality. For one thing, the use of the Erie Canal through Palmyra had been discontinued. The new Barge Canal was in use here, passing by the gravel pit. Barge Canal Lock 29, a short distance west of Palmyra, had been completed. Mud Creek had been deepened and was now being used through here as a part of the Barge Canal.

To load at the gravel dock, which was still in use in the old Erie Canal, our boats were towed a few miles west of the gravel pit. We then locked up on the short level between Barge Canal Locks 29 and 30. This short level had the same elevation as the old Erie Canal, which branched off of the new canal a short way above Lock 29. We were then towed, head first, back to the loading dock in the Erie Canal channel. When the boats were loaded, they were towed west stern first back to where the canals joined. The tug then let go of the stern boat, put its towline on the head boat, and proceeded east in the new canal, which was in use as far as Newark.

Many canal fleets still used animal power in 1913, and tugs furnished by the state were now towing mule or horse-drawn boats from Wayneport to Newark. When the tows reached either of these towns, the animals were put aboard the boats. A tug then towed them over this section of the newly opened Barge Canal, which had no towpath. On arriving at either town, the tug let go of the boats; the animals were put on the towpath, and the boats then continued on over the old section of the canal.

Since we were towed by a tug, the changeover to the new channel did not affect us too much. Although it added about five hours to a round trip, we soon fell into the new routine, after we again started hauling gravel to Poorhouse Lock. Then shortly, we began alternating our trips between there and Lyons. The village of Lyons required many boatloads of gravel because of the numerous Barge Canal structures being erected in the village. At Lyons, Ganargua Creek comes into the Barge Canal just ahead of Lock 27. This required a dam and control gates for the joining of this stream and the Canandaigua Outlet, which forms the Clyde River. Besides the gravel for the lock, concrete abutments were required for a high-level railway bridge that was being built at the lock, which would carry the trolleys of the branch line of the Rochester, Syracuse, and Eastern Railway over the Barge Canal on their way to Canandaigua. There were also long concrete walls to be built at each end of the lock and abutments for two highway bridges in the village.

By the time we finished our trips to this area, we had become quite familiar with Newark and Lyons and the Poorhouse Lock site. We roamed the streets of the villages and had explored the countryside adjacent to the canal. We also spent a lot of our time watching construction work going on at the dam and lock sites.

Another pastime was retrieving spoiled eggs from the canal in the village of Lyons. An incubator chicken-hatching business was conducted in a building with a back entrance close to the canal. On the days the eggs were culled, the bad ones were disposed of by throwing them in the canal, where they floated around until the current carried them away. We recovered those that came near the canal bank and, of course, threw them at anything in sight.

We finished boating gravel to Lyons that fall, and in the spring of 1914 began delivering gravel for Barge Canal Lock 25 at May's Point. (I don't believe any gravel for Lock 26, which is two and a half miles east of Clyde, came from Palmyra. I was told that a nearby pit furnished the gravel for this lock.) May's Point is a small settlement between Clyde and Montezuma. The lock is on the Clyde River and drops boats down about six feet to the level

Erie Canal, Lyons, N. Y.

Lock 55 and the Erie Canal passing by the rear of some business places in the village of Lyons, N.Y.; towpath on left. Photo *circa* 1900. *Buffalo and Erie County Historical Society.*

of the Seneca River. The junction of the two rivers is about two miles east of Lock 25. We ran back and forth between Palmyra and May's Point most of the summer. I was now ten years old and my brother Jim and I were free to roam the countryside while the boats were unloading, which took about two days.

May's Point being sparsely settled, the main attraction for us was fishing and swimming. Walking along the towpath between there and the Seneca River, we could not see a house or a farm building. Both sides of the canal were overgrown with trees and plant life. Nothing was visible other than the canal and towpath. There was an amazing variety of fish in this section of the canal, and it was one of the best fishing grounds we ever came across.

Fishing from the towpath, we caught nice-sized perch, rock bass, sunfish, bullheads, and an occasional blue pike, along with a few chubs and shiners. We fished in many spots along the towpath, and once walked the two miles to the long Richmond aqueduct crossing the Seneca River. Here we tried our luck in the river, catching only one sucker and an eel. Fishing was much better in the canal.

In late summer, with a feeling of regret, we made the last trip to May's Point. Then we started hauling gravel to a small hamlet on the lower long level called Grove Springs, about eight miles west of Rome on the old canal. The main feature here was a canalside store that carried all kinds of merchandise used by canallers. The store was operated by the Wisemantel family for many years. There was a covered spring or well in front of the store, near the edge of the towpath. A wooden suspension type footbridge crossed the canal in front of the store, making it accessible to a few homes on the south side of the canal. A highway bridge crossed the canal a half mile east of the store. All landmarks have now vanished, and Grove Springs today is a part of Stacy's Basin.

Barge Canal Lock 21 and Lock 22 are single locks a mile apart the new canal and two or three miles north of the Grove Springs unloading site. The gravel we unloaded was transported to the construction sites on a narrow-gauge railway on small side-dumping rail cars pulled by a steam dinky engine. The dinky engine ("dinky" compared to a standard-size engine) and cars were well known on construction jobs in the early 1900s and were often used where there were large amounts of material to be moved to a distant site.

Whenever we arrived at Grove Springs, the tug usually ran light to Rome for coal and other supplies, and returned when it was time to start back to the gravel pit. It was all open country around Grove Springs and poor fishing. To while away the two days it took to unload the four boats, we sometimes rode the dinky engine over to the construction sites and watched the building of the locks. We swam in the canal and roamed about the countryside. While wandering around, we once came across a grove of beechnut trees a mile or so from the canal. This section of the state had many nut-bearing beech trees. Soon after a good frost, the small, crescent-shaped nuts fall to the ground. They are easily shelled and make good eating.

A break in the routine for that year occurred when Mother

and we seven children stopped over to visit our Aunt Margaret at Syracuse while Father took the boats on to Grove Springs. Aunt Margaret was a widowed sister of Father's and kept house for herself and a son, Marshal. My brother William, the baby at that time, had been born with a hernia, and Mother believed it urgent for him to have an operation that summer, which was done in a Syracuse hospital during our stopover at Aunt Margaret's. All went well with the operation, and Father, as he had promised, telephoned ahead to tell us when the boats would return through Syracuse. At the end of the fourth day there, we were all glad to get back on the boats at one of the Syracuse locks. While Mother had been going back and forth to the hospital, we were left in the care of our Aunt Margaret. No doubt there were times when we children made it a bit hectic for our Aunt Margaret. She, too, must have been glad to see us return to the boats.

Another thing that occurred on all of the trips to Grove Springs was the trouble we encountered at Gere's Lock. It was #50 on the Erie Canal and was the first lock to be doubled in length in 1884.

Ordinarily, when we came to a lock, the tug went through the single lock at the same time the two head boats went through the double lock. When both were locked down, the tug pulled the first pair of boats from the double lock, then waited a short time for the second pair of boats to be locked down. The two pair of boats were then coupled together and we were soon on our way. However, at Gere's, something had happened to the old double lock. It was narrower than the other locks we passed through. I don't believe it was built that way; possibly one of the lock walls had moved inward from some unexplained pressure.

Returning to Palmyra empty, we could use the double lock. Going to Grove Springs with the boats loaded, we had to use the single lock for the four boats. We could get in the double lock with the loaded boats, but when they were lowered down they would wedge in the lock and could not be moved by the tug, with all the paddle valves open to swell them out. This had been tried, and the boats had to be raised back up and pulled back out of the locks.

At Gere's Lock we had to uncouple the four boats and put them through the single lock. The four single lockings, the uncoupling, and the recoupling consumed much more time, and more hands were needed for this extra work. No matter what time of the day or night we arrived at Gere's Lock with the loaded boats, my brother, Jim, and I were called on to help out. I was an active eleven-year-old then, and what a job my father had waking me up if we arrived at Gere's after midnight. I would wake up and fall back asleep at least four times before my father got me on my feet. Once I was awake, I was a willing hand and helped out wherever I could. I suppose if the double lock at Geres had not been so narrow, I might not have remembered it so well.

The rest of a pleasant and busy season passed quickly going back and forth from Palmyra to Grove Springs. If there were no delays, it took about seven days to make a round trip. This included loading and unloading. We passed through Syracuse and over this section of the canal twice a week, coming and going for the rest of the season.

We had left Tonawanda the first of May and, after being away for seven months, everyone was glad to be homeward bound at the end of the season. I eagerly looked forward to seeing my friends and visiting my boyhood hangouts and thought of going back to school for the winter months.

When we returned to Palmyra, at the beginning of the third season in the spring of 1914, we were surprised about another change that had been made during the winter. The old Erie had been drained through Palmyra. The Barge Canal was in use past the gravel dock. The one-hundred-foot wide embankment between the Barge Canal and older Erie had been removed. A basin had been dug out in front of the loading dock in which the boat could then be loaded. This did away with towing the boats from above Lock 29 down the old canal to the loading dock and then towing them, stern first, back to Lock 29.

At the gravel pit we had often spent some time fishing in the old canal while waiting for the boats to load gravel. But it was not much of a challenging fishing spot. The year the Barge Canal opened opposite the gravel pit, we caught more fish than we could eat. While most of them were young carp, seven to ten inches long, the flesh was firm and sweet and they were good eating. We caught so many that everyone got tired of looking at them. They were easily caught on a hook baited with a wad of bread.

One day while fishing, we saw a snapping turtle swimming about our fishing spot. It would not bite on bread, so we baited the hook with bacon. He took the baited hook quickly, and we hauled him aboard and had turtle chowder the next day. What a job we had beheading that turtle, certainly no job for a novice!

Once while waiting to load, my younger brother, Charles, was paddling around in a borrowed boat when suddenly a calico bass, twelve inches long, leaped out of the water and landed in the boat. My brother was quite elated about this incident and well remembers it to this day. The bass wound up in the frying pan and was a welcome change from carp.

In the meantime we had been steadily hauling gravel to Grove Springs. In midsummer the Grove Springs job was finished, and we began hauling gravel to the Finger Lakes region of the state. The last trip to Grove Springs required only two loads of gravel. There being four boats in the tow, it was decided that the two head boats would take the last two loads to Grove Springs. The second two boats, which were ours, would take two loads to Mud Lock at the foot of Cayuga Lake. To reach Mud Lock, our boats were dropped off at the junction of the Erie and Cayuga-Seneca Canals at Montezuma. The canal with its towpath still in use ran parallel with the east side of the Seneca River from its junction with the Erie Canal to Mud Lock at the foot of Cayuga Lake. Along some sections of the Cayuga-Seneca Canal, one could see the rushes and cat-tails that stretched farther than the eye could see along both banks of the Seneca River.

To save time on this trip with the split loads, it had been arranged for a team of horses to tow our boats from Montezuma to the site of the new lock at the foot of Cayuga Lake, a distance of three or four miles from the junction. On our arrival at Montezuma, a driver and two fine horses were waiting to tow us to our destination.

It was noon on a very hot day and we were soon on our way to the new construction site. The horses had been pulling us along for about an hour, when we noticed something amiss with the team up ahead on the towpath. As the boats drifted toward them, we could see one of the horses lying down on the towpath. It had suffered a sunstroke. A veterinarian was called to look after the animal, but it never recovered. After a delay of a couple of hours, another horse was obtained and we arrived at our destination without further incident.

This was all new country to us. As soon as the boats were tied up, Jim and I were off exploring the surrounding countryside, as well as the foot of Cayuga Lake, and the Seneca River in this vicinity. How well I remember the clearness of the water along the shoreline of the lake. One could see perch, rock bass, an occasional pickerel, and sunfish (or "pumpkin seeds," as they were called in this area). But with the water being clear enough for us to see the fish from where we stood on some small boat docks, the fish must also have been aware of us, for when we dangled a baited hook in front of them, it was ignored. We saw a lot more fish than we caught, though this did not stop us from fishing. We also explored the banks of the river as far as we dared to stray away from where the boats were unloading. On sunny days, every piece of driftwood or rotted log along the river banks was covered its full length with mud turtles sunning themselves. The area teemed with grass snakes and water snakes, snapping turtles, bull frogs, and grass frogs. Many different kinds of water birds also thrived in the swampy areas, including cranes, wild ducks, snipe, kingfishers, sandpipers, and others that I could not name. Those days were adventuresome, busy, and carefree ones for two young boys.

After a number of trips to Mud Lock, which is Lock number one of the four locks on the Cayuga-Seneca branch of the Barge Canal, we began hauling gravel to Seneca Falls for Lock 2 and Lock 3. Later on, we also hauled gravel to Lock 4 at Waterloo.

On one of our trips to Seneca Falls, with gravel for the two flight locks being built there, my younger brother, Charles, had a close call. It was early in the fall and our boats were tied to the sloped canal bank because of a fast current in the canalized Seneca River, after a heavy rainfall. At noon time we were all down in the cabin eating when young Charles came in soaking wet and looking very scared. He had fallen overboard and had managed to get out by himself. Luckily, he had fallen in between the boats and the sloped canal bank.

When asked how he had got out of the water, he told us he had sunk under water until he touched the sloped canal bank; then, he had simply crawled up the bank under water until he came up on dry land, and came back aboard the boats. He gave all of us a bad scare because no one had seen or heard him fall in the water. Had he fallen in on the other side of the boat, the current would have carried him away, as the seven-year-old was still unable to swim. He told me later on that he fell in the canal again the next day while walking across a plank, but was able to hang on to the plank and did not go under water. Again he got out by himself.

On another occasion that same year, what could have been a serious accident happened to my younger sister. She had gone on deck with Mother to bring some articles in to the cabin from the deck box. After getting some vegetables, she stepped too far backward and tumbled into the six-foot-deep empty midship. She was brought to the cabin and remained unconscious so long that Mother thought she had suffered a brain concussion, but after what seemed a very long time, she came to and suffered no ill effects from the fall. She had simply had the wind knocked out of her.

We ended up the season still making runs to Seneca Falls. In the spring of 1915, my brother Jim and I stayed at home with Mother and the rest of the family, for Mother would have another child in a few months, and our family was outgrowing the limited accommodations onboard the old canal boats. Father reluctantly left for Palmyra with the boats when the canal opened early in May.

Jim and I were not too happy about being left at home. Father must have missed us, too, for as soon as school let out it was arranged for us to join him on the boats. We took the train to Palmyra and arrived there just as the boats were returning to the gravel pit. The wife of the steersman was taking care of the cooking, and we looked forward to a carefree summer on the old boats. We helped out where we could by keeping the cook supplied with firewood and water. We cleaned the boats up after loading and unloading and were always on deck at Gere's lock, and also helped to keep the boats pumped out.

The boats were still running to Seneca Falls, and we spent most of our time fishing, swimming, and exploring the countryside at each end of the trip. On a return trip to Palmyra we found a homemade rowboat adrift in the canal; catching hold of it with a pike pole, we pulled it aboard the boats.

Now more than ever, we got around to different fishing

spots. No matter what side of the canal or river we were tied up to we got to the other side with the old rowboat. After having the rowboat for some time, we neglected to pull it aboard the canal boats when we left Palmyra. It was left pulled up on the river bank near the gravel pit. When we returned, it had disappeared.

The season passed quickly for us and much too soon for Father. Each time the boats arrived at the gravel dock, they were tied up in the Barge Canal and were moved in and out of the loading basin as they were needed. But Barge Canal construction work was nearing completion, and we finished boating gravel from Palmyra about October 1915. Most of the work still to be done for the Barge Canal consisted of dredging and deepening the channels.

This was the shortest season the boats had worked in four or five years. Father was not happy with the early finish. It had been a poor year financially, and there was no work in sight for the boats for the next season.

None of the boatmen became rich in the gravel trade at Palmyra. The boats were paid so much a cubic yard for carrying the gravel; the price varied according to the distance it was hauled. Fifty percent of the boats' earnings went to the tug for towing. But out of the other half, the boat owner must pay a steersman ($60 a month and board), and buy tie-up lines and other equipment needed to operate the boats and keep them in good repair. Every few years the boats had to be drydocked and have their bottoms recaulked and any necessary underwater repairs made, and they had to be repainted each year. At the end of the season, a boater was lucky to have a few hundred dollars to tide him and his family over the winter. Besides all of this, he had to look after the boats and keep them securely tied up and pumped out through the winter months.

When spring came around, he usually owed the grocer, and got the boats ready for work by using his credit to fit them out with the necessary supplies and equipment needed to get them started when canal navigation opened.

CHAPTER 14

A Brief Return to Lumber Boating

I T WAS nearly the first of June before there were any prospects of work for our two old canal boats in 1916. It promised to be a slow year; and, as it turned out, this year was the next to last season that animal power would be used on the New York State canals.

The demise of the older Erie Canal would take place at the end of 1917, as the Barge Canal took over. There was very little work in sight for our type of boats, which had been converted so as to accommodate the hauling of stone and gravel for Barge Canal construction work.

Near the end of May, we were towed to Lockport, where our boats were put in the drydock for some caulking and underwater repairs. This would ready them for a job of hauling gravel from Tonawanda to Lockport and Gasport for new road construction in that area. This job, Father had learned, would begin the middle of June and take about two months.

While the boats were in the drydock, I became acquainted with some boys who came each noon hour from school to swim in the creek below the drydock. Their "swimming hole" was six to eight feet deep and about twenty feet wide. One noon time, I had been in swimming with the gang and, while some of the other boys and I were getting dressed, my attention was drawn to a boy about nine years old, who was floundering in the middle of the creek. I saw him go under once and come splashing to the surface. Since I was the oldest boy in the group, all eyes turned to me. Not without some misgivings, I quickly threw off most of my clothes, dove in, and reached the boy before he went under for the last time. While swimming back to the shore with him under one arm, my head was under more times than it was above water. I was thankful that the creek was not very wide at this particular swimming spot. When I realized that it was up to me to do the rescuing, more than one thought flashed through my mind: Will the drowning boy get a stranglehold on me and pull me under? Can I make it back to shore with him? Would I ever after regret it if I did not try to save him? Well, needless to say, I have always been glad that I decided to try, and he came through unscathed, even though I never did find out his name.

Soon after leaving the drydock, we started out on the Lockport-Gasport road construction job. The few months of hauling gravel passed quickly, and afterwards, for the first time since we owned the boats they were lying idle in Tonawanda in the middle of the boating season.

No work was in sight for the boats. But, unexpectedly, an old acquaintance of Father's got news of three boatloads of lumber to be shipped to Albany early in October. This boatman had kept his boats in the lumber trade continuously while we were hauling gravel. He was also idle and had two teams of mules but only one canal boat. His other boat had been damaged beyond repair in an accident, and he did not replace it because the end of the Erie Canal operation was only a year away.

He told Father of the prospective shipment of three boatloads of white pine to Albany, and between them they contracted to carry the shipments. His mules would do the towing, expenses would be shared, and whatever profit was made on the trip would be divided equally.

Although our boats were quite old, they had been kept up and were still sound enough to carry lumber. So, hoping to make a few more dollars with the old boats, Father decided to go back in the lumber trade. With no other work to be had, it was that or nothing. Our two boats still had the false or stone decks, which had been installed when they were put in for the gravel trade. We got busy and removed the old wooden false decks, which were rotted and about used up anyway, and Father had the boats ready

An upbound light tow passing a tow going in the same direction. Drawing by
E. Mayes.

in plenty of time to load the lumber. Even though our boats were originally built to carry lumber, I never expected to see them back in the lumber trade again.

The lumber shipment arrived from the lakes on schedule. With the three boats loaded with lumber, we left Tonawanda at the end of the first week in October, figuring we had plenty of time to go to Albany, unload, and return to Tonawanda for the winter.

Two drivers were hired; my father and the other boat owner handled the steering. I was the handy man on the third boat, ready to fill in wherever I was needed. I sometimes worked as the driver, was always on hand at changing time, held the wheel while the steersman was eating, kept the boats pumped out, cut firewood for the cook, and made myself generally useful.

By 1916, as I have explained before, certain parts of the Barge Canal were in use, and the State furnished tug service for the canal boats wherever the towpath had been eliminated. Tugs towed us a good part of the way on this trip, but where the towpath was intact, we used our mules.

For some reason, having the mules aboard the boats again added something that was missing all those years when we towed by tugs. While the animals required considerable care, looking after them and stopping to change teams every six hours was looked forward to, as it broke up the monotony on long stretches of the canal.

One of the teams consisted of three white mules, two of average size and a small mule that could be very ornery at times. For no reason, whenever he was in the bowstable, he would start kicking. He had the rear end of that bowstable shattered and almost kicked out before we reached Albany. I sometimes wondered if that mule maybe had a toothache. When changing mules one evening at seven o'clock on the upper long level, we were tied up on the sloped bank of the canal. When this ornery, smallest mule was led over the horse bridge from the boat to the towpath, he stopped in the middle of the bridge and started kicking his hind legs up in the air. He lost his balance and fell off into the canal. Though he was led up the sloped bank to the towpath without much trouble, he had his ears down flat to his head and his tail between his legs. He was shivering when we hitched him up to the towline and he pulled for some time before his ears rose and his tail lifted. But we had no more trouble with him at changing time after that ducking in the canal on that cool October evening.

Another incident concerning this same mule happened at a midday changing time. While I was leading him into position for the driver to hitch him up to the whiffletrees, he stumbled and his front hoof came down on my canvass-shod foot and smashed my big toe. From then on, I had a particular dislike for that small mule.

We towed with the mules from Tonawanda to Wayneport, a small hamlet a few miles east of Fairport. Here the team of mules was put aboard the boats and a tug towed us to Newark, a distance of seventeen miles over a completed section of the Barge Canal, which had no towpath. At Newark, the tug let go, and we again used our mules on through Syracuse and over the lower long level. From here, we continued in the old Erie Canal to Little Falls, then used tugs over the Mohawk River nearly to Cohoes, when we again used the old Erie the rest of the way to Albany. Passing through Cohoes and Watervliet, one could see that the use of the Erie Canal would soon end. Here the occupants of many buildings bordering on the canal edge had been dumping rubbish in the channel, and it was just about passable.

We had encountered many delays by waiting for tugs and by high water in the Mohawk River. We finally arrived at the Lumber District in Albany, where we found the old horse-drawn trolley was still running. The unloading of the boats was slow, and we did not start back for Tonawanda until the early part of November. When we arrived at Frankfort, ice had begun to form in the canal. Our progress was rather slow because of the three-boat tow, which required more time at the locks. Cold weather had set in early. Father and the other boat owner, whose mules were towing us, did not think we would reach Tonawanda before the canal froze up.

The old wooden canal boats would not withstand towing through ice, even one-quarter inch thick, for it chewed the planking and pulled the oakum out of seams. After talking it over with his partner, Father decided to leave our two boats at Frankfort for the winter. The mules and the single boat, interestingly enough now, as I look back, went on and made it to Tonawanda.

Father and I spent a day or two in Frankfort securing the

Two animal-towed fleets about to meet and pass each other. Drawing by
E. Mayes.

boats for the winter. They were left tied up on the outside of an old canal boat on which an elderly couple, a Mr. and Mrs. Brown, made their home. The Browns agreed to look after our boats until spring, and we then took a train for home.

That winter was uneventful and, in the spring of 1917, about the first of May, Father and I returned to Frankfort to bring the boats back to Tonawanda. When we arrived at the boats, we were greeted by Mr. and Mrs. Brown, who had taken good care of everything. But we were disappointed to find the canal empty and the boats resting on the bottom of the canal. Upon inquiring when the canal would be filled, we were told by the State Canal Authority that this section of the old canal had been discontinued, and that the Barge Canal, a short distance north of Frankfort, was now in use.

We were informed that, in about two weeks, water would be let in to this section of the canal where our boats lay. The State was building a junction lock at Mohawk, New York, which would allow boats to lock from the Barge Canal into the former Erie Canal channel at this point. This section of the Erie Canal was to be kept open between Mohawk and Utica to serve area industries.

There was nothing for us to do but wait. We had cleaned up and aired the cabin and the bedding of the after boat, made a fire in the stove, washed up the dishes and pots and pans, made up the bunks, and prepared to live on the boats while waiting. Not caring about cooking, Father assigned me to that task. Variety was not a part of our menus. Boiled or fried eggs, toast and coffee for breakfast, mostly baloney sandwiches, or hamburgs, and tea for lunch. I fried pork chops, boiled potatoes, and made tea for our supper on the old black, wood-burning cabin stove. While eating, a teakettle of water was heating on the stove to wash the dishes. I did not mind the cooking job, because it gave me something to do and helped to pass the time; and I did learn a little about the culinary art. If the food was burnt or underdone, my dad never complained. I think he would have put up with most anything rather than do the cooking himself.

The cabin floor sloped because the boats were resting on the bottom of the empty canal. We were always walking uphill or downhill when moving about the cabin, but we soon got used to it; any kind of shelter is better than being in the open.

A few hundred feet from where the Browns made their home, another old canal boat housed a family of four school-age children and their widowed mother, who worked to support the family. As time passed slowly waiting for the canal to be filled, I became acquainted with this family—the Johnsons—and often went fishing with Mrs. Johnson's two boys.

It was a common thing at that time for low-income families to make their home on old canal boats or house boats, not only at Frankfort, but in many towns along the canal and in Buffalo. Some people even built living quarters on large floats or rafts which could not sink and required no pumping. This mode of living attracted some people because no rent or taxes had to be paid. The Canal authorities never seemed to object to people living on old boats or rafts along the canal as long as the boats were tied up in wide places in the canal and on the heelpath side and did not interfere with the passage of canal craft. This type of living along the New York State waterways disappeared when the Barge Canal came into use.

Hearing nothing at the end of two weeks, Father again made inquiries and was told it would be another two weeks before the junction lock at Mohawk would be finished. Then, after all this wait, the next time we inquired about the progress of the lock, we were told that the junction lock project, although partly finished, had been abandoned. To say the least, this bit of news was quite a shock. The boats were permanently stranded on the bottom of the empty canal. Four weeks of waiting had been wasted, and money had been borrowed to bring the boats back to Tonawanda. We were dejected and disappointed, but there was nothing to do but leave the fully equipped boats and go home to Tonawanda.

In all fairness, we felt that we should have been told, in the spring of 1917, that the canal at Frankfort was being abandoned. An appeal was made to State for the loss of the boats, but it was unsuccessful. Ruling on the grounds that the canal was a toll-free waterway, the State determined that it was not liable for damage or loss of any craft using the canal.

That was the last we saw of the old canal boats named for Martin Hyde and Sol Goldsmith.

CHAPTER 15

On the Niagara Frontier

S OON AFTER returning home in June 1917, Father and I went to work for Benjamin L. Cowles, a fleet owner and operator of a small shipyard in Buffalo, who was also the owner of a number of canal-size tugs and some old stone- and gravel-carrying canal boats. Mr. Cowles had tugs towing gravel boats at Palmyra a few years before our boats were working there.

We were put in charge of two canal boats engaged in hauling stone paving block and some curbstone from Hulberton to Buffalo, to the yard of the International Railway Company on Scajacquada Creek.

The old canal boats also carried slag from the Wickwire Steel plant in the Town of Tonawanda for road construction in Erie County. The crushed slag was loaded on the boats in the Erie Canal at the Wickwire plant between Tonawanda and Black Rock. We boated a number of loads to a spot on the Niagara River just below Edgewater on Grand Island and, also, along the canal between Tonawanda and Pendleton. Today, this kind of hauling would be done by truck.

On preceding pages, mention is made of Niagara River gravel. When concrete came into general use, gravel, grit, sand, and cement comprised the mixture made into concrete.

A good grade of clean gravel and grit was to be had from a five- or six-mile stretch of the east branch of the Niagara River, from Riverside Park to the Grand Island bridges. The gravel and

Eight head of mules towing two partly loaded boats between Hudson and
Genesee Streets, Buffalo, N.Y. The fastest current or flow of water along the
Erie Canal was between Tonawanda and Buffalo. Canal men put all their
stock on the towpath at Tonawanda when going west with loaded boats over
this section of the canal. Photo *circa* 1912. *Buffalo and Erie County Historical Society.*

grit deposits came from Lake Erie, being washed from the lake
during periods of high wind storms and strong currents.

Each workday morning in the navigation season, if you were
on the Niagara River's east branch, six or seven sandboats (or
"Sandsuckers," as they were called) could be seen pumping along
or near the shores of the river.

Three or four companies had gravel yards in this area, and it
was a sizable industry. I believe the business came into being in the
1890s, and lasted until sometime in the 1930s, when pumping
gravel from the Niagara River came to a halt.

Fishing in the river had dwindled over the years, and conservationists believed the sandsuckers were destroying the fish eggs deposited in the river bed. They petitioned the State and were successful in having a law passed that prohibited sandsuckers from operating in the Niagara River. Meanwhile, the gravel companies were given time to acquire and convert lake vessels for pumping the material from Lake Erie. Within the next ten years or so, conservationists were again successful in having a law passed that prohibited sandsuckers from operating in New York State territorial waters on Lake Erie.

In between boating slag and paving stone, with the old canal boats, we occasionally "lightered" (partly unloaded) pulpwood steamers, which came through the Welland Canal from Canada. The ships were loaded to twelve-foot draft and had to be lightered to ten feet to proceed down the west branch of the Niagara River to the city of Niagara Falls.

The pulpwood-laden steamships tied up below the shiplock at Black Rock. Here, the two canal boats were placed alongside and were loaded from the steamers, which were equipped with cargo handling cranes or booms. When the steamer had been lightered up to ten-foot draft, it proceeded down the river with the two canal boats lashed alongside. At Niagara Falls, the pulpwood was unloaded into a large log boom anchored in the Niagara River near Schlosser's Landing. This large boom of pulpwood was made up into smaller booms, which were then towed to a pond on the river's edge by a tug owned and operated by the paper company. A conveyor removed the pulpwood from the water and placed it on a huge storage pile for the use of the International Paper Company's Buffalo Avenue paper mill in the city of Niagara Falls.

Near the end of that summer, a steamer loaded with pulpwood had capsized at Port Dalhousie, spilling its deckload into the harbor. In 1917, this was still the northern terminus of the Welland Canal.

A tug and two canal boats were sent there to be loaded with the pulpwood, which had been removed from the water, to deliver it to Niagara Falls. Father and I were on the two canal boats. Although I did not know it at the time, we followed the same route to Port Dalhousie that was used by sailing vessels plying the first Welland Canal completed in 1829.

Canada's first Welland Canal was built in 1824-29 from Port

View of the Erie Basin between Genesee and Court Streets, Buffalo, N.Y., showing a number of canal grain boats light and loaded. Behind is a whaleback lake steamer unloading grain at the wooden exchange elevator, with a fuel scow alongside. Because of their shape the whalebacks were also called pigboats by the sailors. They were also known as MacDougall's dream because they were designed and first built by Alexander MacDougall in 1888. The last one to sail the Great Lakes was the *Meteor,* used as an oil tanker until the 1970s; it is now a museum ship at Superior, Wisc. Photo *circa* 1896. *Buffalo and Erie County Historical Society.*

Dalhousie to Port Robinson, Ontario. The canal had an eight-foot draft, forty wooden locks, and was 110 feet long by 22 feet wide. Vessel cargo capacity was 165 tons.

The canal was opened by the passage of two schooners, the *Anne and Jane* of Upper Canada and the American Schooner, *R. H. Boughton,* of Youngstown, New York. Departing from Port Dalhousie on November 27, they were delayed by ice in the canal and locks, and one of the schooners was grounded temporarily. Arriving at Port Robinson, they locked down into the Welland River, then along that river to Chippawa and up the Niagara River and into Lake Erie, through a shiplock at Black Rock. The lock was completed in 1824 and formed a functional part of the first Welland Canal until 1833. The vessels arrived in Buffalo on December 2, where they were given a hearty welcome and returned homeward the next day.

Sailing vessels were the new canal's main traffic; they were towed by oxen through the canal, which had two towpaths—one for upbound vessels and one for downbound vessels.

By 1833, the Welland Canal was extended to Port Colborne, Ontario, on Lake Erie. This shortened the route and eliminated the use of the Welland and Niagara Rivers for vessels passing through the canal. This must have also eliminated some sizable towing bills for owners of sailing vessels, as I don't believe they could pass up or down the Welland or Niagara Rivers without the assistance of towboats. After 1833, the lock at Port Robinson and the route down the Welland River to Chippawa and the Niagara were kept in use. In the 1850s, steamboats operating over this route on a regular schedule were carrying freight between Port Dalhousie and Buffalo. Transportation over this route ended when the railroads became established and captured the freight business.

The second Welland Canal was completed in 1845. There were 27 stone locks, 150 feet long by 27 feet wide. Vessels up to 140 feet long, with nine-foot draft and carrying 750 tons of cargo, could pass through. The third canal was finished in 1887 and allowed vessels up to a length of 255 feet, with a maximum cargo of 2,700 tons to pass through at twelve feet draft. It took a different route to Allanburg than the second one did, but the same route from Allanburg to Lake Erie.

The Welland Ship Canal was the fourth canal; started in 1913, it was not completed until 1932-33. The canal has eight locks which accommodate vessels up to 750 feet long by 75 feet wide, with a draft of 25 feet, which allows the passage of vessels carrying 25,000 tons.

Since the completion of the fourth Welland Canal, Port Dalhousie is no longer the northern terminus. It has been changed to

Port Weller, which is about three miles eastward on Lake Ontario. It is 27.6 miles from Port Weller to Port Colborne on Lake Erie. The Welland Ship Canal permits the passage of foreign vessels traveling via the St. Lawrence Seaway to upper Great Lakes ports, where they can unload or load and are then able to navigate nonstop to ports all over the world.

In taking the two canal boats to Port Dalhousie in 1917 to "rescue" the load of pulpwood from the capsized steamer, we would be taking the same route taken by boaters on the first Welland Canal. We proceeded from Buffalo down the west branch of the Niagara River to Chippawa, a village on the Canadian shore about a mile above the Falls; here we entered Chippawa Creek, which joined the Welland River a short way from the village. I recall that I had quite a thrill as we entered the creek, because I could see the spray rising from the Falls; I also felt relieved that the tug had not broken down as we arrived there, fearing that we might have been carried over the Falls.

On our way to Port Robinson, via Chippawa Creek and the Welland River, we passed through some swing bridges operated by hand power. To my surprise, the bridges and the junction lock at Port Robinson were operated by women. This reminded me that it was 1917 and that Canada, along with Great Britain, had been engaged in World War I since 1914. There was a shortage of Canadian manpower, and wherever they could, the women filled the gap.

From Port Robinson, we proceeded down the Welland Canal to Port Dalhousie, where the pulpwood from the capsized freighter was piled on the dock and we tied up for the night. The next day, a large gang of men began loading the pulpwood into the boats by hand. They finished loading us that afternoon, and the next day we returned to Niagara Falls. The boats were unloaded, also by hand labor, into the International Paper Company's pulpwood boom anchored in the Niagara River.

It had been a short trip of three days, but it had been a whole new experience for me. It was my first time out of the United States, and my first trip on the Welland Canal. It was also the first time I was afloat so near the mighty Cataract.

The west branch of the Niagara River is no longer a navigable channel, having been discontinued by the Corps of Engineers, and

A tug and two canal boats about to enter Chippawa Creek from the Niagara River at village of Chippawa, Ontario. Drawing by E. Mayes.

there are no buoys or other aids to navigation in the old channel.

Prior to the abandonment of the branch, westbound cargoes

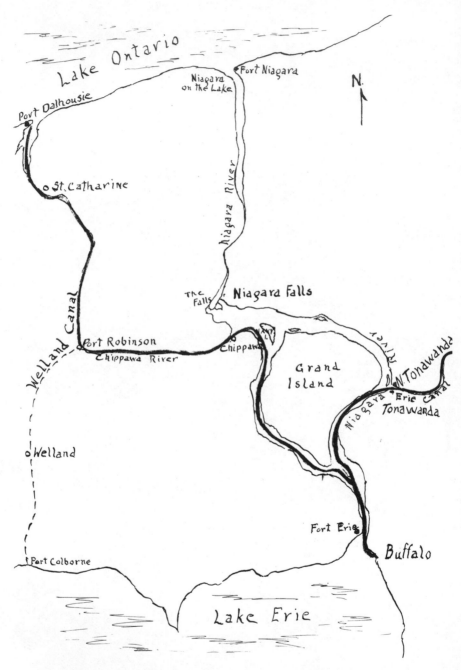

Map showing the course of a tug and two canal boats from Buffalo to Chippawa, via the Niagara River.

for Niagara Falls, arriving at Tonawanda via the Barge Canal, had to be towed up the river to Buffalo, and then down the west branch to their destination. In the 1930s, a more direct and better channel from Tonawanda to Niagara Falls, via the east branch of the Niagara River, was completed and is still in use.

Another short, but historic, waterway in the Buffalo area is Scajacquada Creek; although only a small section of it was navigable, this creek played an important part in the early history of Black Rock and Buffalo. Originally, the creek emptied directly into the Niagara River. Near its mouth, on the west bank of the creek, was a shipyard that built the side-wheel steamer, *Walk-in-the-Water.* Launched in 1807, it was the first steamship on the upper Great Lakes.

The current in the two-mile stretch of the Niagara River, between the site of the former shipyard and Lake Erie, is very swift. About opposite Massachusetts Avenue, it attains a speed of seven or eight miles per hour. The new steamship, having insufficient power to breast the current, was assisted to reach the lake by a number of oxen on the end of a towline. Some onlookers at that time, who probably thought nothing would replace sail, described the assistance as "a horned breeze."

A great part of the War of 1812 was fought on the Niagara Frontier, and Buffalo figured prominently in that conflict. Ships being of prime importance, the United States government took over Captain Asa Stannard's shipyard at the mouth of Scajacquada Creek. It was at this Navy Yard that five ships of Commodore Perry's fleet were reconditioned for his glorious victory over the British on Lake Erie. The battle was fought on September 10, 1813.

Near the foot of Massachusetts Avenue, and extending out into the Niagara River, was the Black Rock from which the village took its name. It was blasted out of the way when the Erie Canal came through this area. The coming of the canal also raised the level of Scajacquada Creek about four feet, and it then emptied into the canal. The creek was made navigable a short distance past Niagara Street. No doubt canal craft served industries along this short section of Scajacquada Creek in earlier days. I first became acquainted with the creek in 1916-17 by going into it on canal boats loaded with paving blocks and curbstone.

Looking north from the Ferry Street bridge, Buffalo, N.Y. The vessel with the high superstructure is a floating grain elevator, which could unload grain from one vessel to another or store 30,000 bushels in its hold. The wall or land strip to the left separating Black Rock Harbor from the canal was removed in 1905 to make way for the Barge Canal. The Queen City Mills burned June 18, 1901. Note towpath on right. Photo *circa* 1890s. *Buffalo and Erie County Historical Society.*

While animal power was still in use on the Erie Canal, there was a bridge along the towpath spanning Scajacquada Creek just east of Forest Avenue. It was of the same type that carried the mules across the drydock entrance at Lockport. It was also mounted on wheels and had to be winched out of the way on a track when boats entered or left the creek.

Almost from its beginning and up to the end of trolley cars in Buffalo streets, the International Railway Company had a storage yard along the south shore of Scajacquada Creek, between Niagara Street and West Avenue. Under its franchise, the trolley line had to pave and maintain the pavement which covered its right of way through the streets of Buffalo and other towns or cities through which it operated.

Here canal boats unloaded paving blocks and curbstone brought from the Medina and Hulberton sandstone quarries. The storage yard also contained a large pile of gravel, dredged from the Niagara River, and a pile of yellow sand that came from the Canadian side of Lake Erie. The sand was dried and used on the street car tracks to increase traction in wet or icy weather.

The trolley line had a spur track running off of the main line on Niagara Street so that work trains could load the paving material and gravel on flat or dump cars. An electric-powered derrick or crane unloaded the incoming material from the boats and also loaded the outgoing material on work trains.

In the fall of 1917, I started decking and firing on small tugs. I liked machinery and had decided that I would become a "Tug Engineer." The winter was routine, and I worked part time watching some marine equipment that had been tied up in the Erie Canal a short distance from our house in Tonawanda.

In the spring of 1918, I was employed as a fireman-deckhand on a small steam tug at $75 per month for a twelve-hour work day. The tug was hired to tow some shallow-draft dredging equipment that was to do some unfinished work between Tonawanda and Pendleton for the completion of the Barge Canal.

The work could not be finished until that spring, as the Erie Canal had been kept in operation until the end of the 1917 canal season. In the winter of 1917-18 the old Tonawanda Dam was removed, and the New York Central Railway bridge that crossed Tonawanda Creek just west of the dam had been raised to allow canal craft to pass under a temporary span. Starting about April 1, we towed the equipment to the different work areas. The job lasted about six weeks and was finished in time for the opening of the Barge Canal.

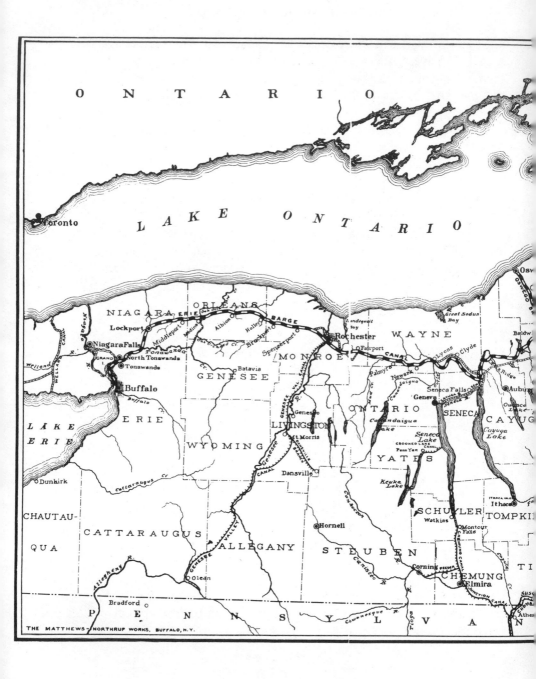

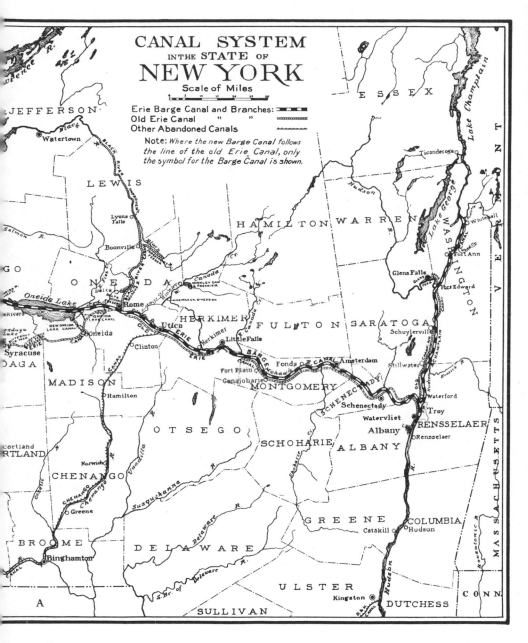

CANAL SYSTEM
IN THE STATE OF
NEW YORK
Scale of Miles

Erie Barge Canal and Branches:
Old Erie Canal   "   "
Other Abandoned Canals

Note: *Where the new Barge Canal follows the line of the old Erie Canal, only the symbol for the Barge Canal is shown.*

Reproduced from Buffalo Historical Society Publications, XII (1908)

CHAPTER 16

The Opening of the Barge Canal

T HE BARGE CANAL opened in the spring of 1918 under government control. We were then, along with our allies, at war with Germany. The War Department appointed the United States Railroad Administration to control and operate the new canal, which it did during the years 1918 and 1919. Canal operation was still under management of the War Department in 1920.

During its first three years of operation, the new canal did help to relieve a railroad car shortage prevalent at the time. It carried many tons of war and relief supplies from the Great Lakes area to the Atlantic Seaboard, destined for wartorn Europe. It is generally believed, however, that the new canal could have done much better for those first years had it been under other management. Shippers reported that government barges were in transit as long as seventy-five days from Buffalo to New York. There were also reports that government barges with cargo valued at hundreds of thousands of dollars, on which shippers were paying interest charges, laid at the Barge Canal terminal in Albany for several weeks.

When the canal opened, few tugs or towboats of suitable draft and power were available for canal use. The government rented or chartered what tugs were to be had. I recall that they also took over two tugs for canal use from companies whose operation depended on this part of their equipment. One was the steel steam tug *Wm. D. Kropp,* owned and operated by the Grand

The tug *Crescent* with a loaded Barge Canal tow on a long hawser. This tug and the *Lotta L. Cowles* were former Lake Erie fish tugs, converted to Barge Canal towboats by the Cowles Towing Co. The after-raised section of deckhouse was added on for the galley. The crew slept below decks in the forward end of the tug. Photo *circa* 1920s. *Buffalo and Erie County Historical Society.*

Island Ferry Company. The tug towed a barge which carried vehicles across the Niagara River between Tonawanda and Grand Island. The takeover of the tug left lower Grand Island without ferry service for many months, until an outmoded wooden tug was purchased to replace the *Kropp,* which was never returned to the Ferry Company.

Also taken over was the steel steam tug *Phillip T. Dodge,* owned and operated by the International Paper Company at Niagara Falls. The paper mill received its pulpwood shipments from Canada by lake steamers. The steamers unloaded in a pulpwood boom anchored in the Niagara River. The tug was used for towing pulpwood from the boom to the shoreside paper mill. The government takeover of the tug ended waterborne shipments of pulpwood to Niagara Falls. Thereafter, the mill received its pulpwood shipments by rail.

There were not many new barges in operation on the new Barge Canal during the first season. This was due to the fact that fleet operators and boat builders were not sure just what type of wooden barges would be best suited for the Barge Canal, and steel was not available to private boat builders because of the war. A number of new and slightly different types of wooden barges had been built at Cohoes and other boatyards in that area. They were not too unlike the Erie Canal boats, except that they had stave bows which were planked straight up and down with rounded corners and, of course, had no bowstables. They were dry cargo boats with hatch-covered cargo holds designed for the grain trade. The boats had been built for individual owners and small fleet operators who had owned and operated boats on the Erie Canal. The new boats were from 21 to 23 feet wide by 108 feet long with 12-foot sides. They were of 600 ton capacity and carried 20,000 bushels of grain. This was 2½ times the capacity of the Erie Canal boats. During the first few years of Barge Canal operation, there was an unusual number of grain barges sunk along the canal, as well as on Oneida Lake. When a sinking occurred, the wooden barge, as well as the cargo, was usually a total loss because the wet grain swelled up and split the barge open. The accidents hampered canal operation and were costly to insurance companies. Many of the sinkings and other accidents were due to the fact that towboats were still using a long towline or hawser on the larger and faster-moving Barge Canal tows, along with the same steering apparatus that had been used on the smaller animal-towed Erie Canal boats. This type of man-powered steering gear had been ideal for the Erie Canal, but such gear did not have enough power for a steersman to properly guide the Barge Canal tows pulled by steam-powered towboats between guard gate piers and bridge abutments on long towlines with the old-fashioned steering gears. Some boats were sunk by striking the ends of lock walls, especially during periods of high water and fast current, when trying to enter a lock. I don't recall what year it was but New York State eventually passed a ruling that all canal tows were to use two shorter 100-foot tow lines, one on each corner of the head barge, instead of the simple 300-foot towline that had been in use. Although the shorter towlines slowed the progress of the canal tows slightly,

The wooden steam tug *Lotta L. Cowles* and Barge Canal tow eastbound on the canalized Oneida River. The two head boats are the wooden stave-bowed, 500-ton type barges put in use when the Barge Canal opened in 1918. The three rear boats are Erie Canal size. All five boats and the tug locked through at one time. Photo *circa* 1920s. *Buffalo and Erie County Historical Society.*

they enabled the towboat to help guide the tow of boats at all times and sharply reduced the collisions and sinkings.

Today, there are few, if any, hawser tows on the Barge Canal. Most of the commercial traffic is oil tank barges shoved and guided by a pusher tug, rigidly connected to the stern of the barge.

During the first few years of Barge Canal operation, there were a number of the Erie steam canal fleets in service and also many of the small-size Erie Canal boats, three of which were put in tow with two of the new and larger Barge Canal boats. This made up a five-boat tow, and, along with a tug, the fleet almost completely filled the new canal locks. The average time for a loaded tow of that size between Buffalo and Waterford was seven days. Eight days was the average time between these points for two animal-towed boats on the old Erie. The tug usually returned to Buffalo with empty boats, taking from four and a half to five days, with the same type of tow.

An example of the increase in size and capacity of the Barge Canal over the Erie can be had by this description of a steam canal

A diesel tug and a tow of loaded barges headed for Buffalo. This section of the Barge Canal is the deep land cut between Pendleton and the rock cut above Lockport. Photo *circa* 1940.

fleet that was in use on the Erie Canal and the same fleet con-verted to Barge Canal use. On the Erie, the fleet consisted of a four-boat unit. The steamer and pushboat (or "consort," as it was often called) were coupled together in a rigid manner that allowed the steamer to steer itself and the pushboat. Two canal boats towed on a long hawser or towline made up the rest of the tow. The four boats required two lockings of two boats at a time in the lengthened locks of the Erie Canal.

On the Barge Canal, two more Erie Canal size boats were added to the steam canal fleet. This made up a six-boat unit that could all be locked through a Barge Canal lock at one time. The

Erie Canal, Montezuma, N.Y. Note the footbridge crossing the canal in the foreground. To save footsteps there were quite a number of footbridges along the canal before the automobile became popular.

five boats and the steamer lying two abreast in the lock used all but ten feet of the available 300-foot length, and about two-thirds of the 44½-foot width.

The term "consort" was heard now and then when referring to steam canal boat fleets, which made their first appearance on the Erie in 1870. I believe the term was used because the steamer and its fleet were seldom separated. The steamer, its pushboat, and the two boats it towed on a long hawser or towline were a unit that traveled up and down the canal and the Hudson River, season after season. The extended use of the Erie steam canal boat fleets has a comparison in history with the once popular Durham boat that was used on the Mohawk River and other natural waterways of New York State before the Erie Canal, for the Durham boats also were used on the first Erie until they were replaced by the larger and more efficient Erie Canal boats.

The steam canal fleets and the smaller boats built for the Erie Canal were kept busy and put to good use in 1918 and during the European postwar recovery period, but gradually they disappeared as new and larger boats came into use on the Barge Canal.

There were two large and expensive engineering features related to the Barge Canal not known or seen by the casual traveler and boatman passing along the waterway.

The new Rome summit level required a greater supply of water than was available from the sources which had supplied water to the old Erie Canal summit level. The new sources developed in connection with Barge Canal construction are the headwaters of the Mohawk River and West Canada Creek. The building of reservoirs on these headwaters added two new lakes to the map of the State.

The waters of the upper Mohawk are held in storage at the Delta Reservoir, or Delta Lake as the people in the vicinity prefer to call it. This is situated about five miles north of Rome and occupies a basin formed by an enlargement of the river valley just above a rock-walled gorge.

The dam which holds back the water in this reservoir is about 1,100 feet long, with a spillway 300 feet long near its center. Its height is 100 feet from crest to its lowest foundation. The concrete apron is 10 feet below the river bottom, so that a permanent pool of that depth is maintained to act as a water cushion to break the erosive force of the water in its fall of about 70 feet to the surface of the pool. The reservoir submerged 10 miles of highway, seven Black River canal locks, and one aqueduct, and required the removal of 295 buildings. The relocation of nearly two miles of Black River Canal, including four new locks and an aqueduct, was necessary. Incidently, the reservoir has considerable influence, today, in mitigating disastrous flood conditions in the lower Mohawk Valley.

The second of these two new sources of supply was West Canada Creek, which reaches the Mohawk Valley in the vicinity of Herkimer, too far below the Rome summit level to be of any material use. To make it available where needed, therefore, a diverting channel was constructed to take the water after it comes from an impounding reservoir some five miles by way of the creek and turn it across a rather low divide into the channel of Nine Mile Creek, whence it flows by natural stream to the Barge Canal, reaching it near Oriskany. The reservoir, known by the name of the village near which it is situated, Hinckly, is about twenty miles north of Utica and lies in the foothills of the Adirondack mountains. Building the Hinckly necessitated the removal of 209 build-

A steel three-section, bolted-together, self-propelled empty grain barge passing through the Tonawandas. Two of them owned by the Cargill Grain Co.
were once in use on the Barge Canal. Photo *circa* 1930. *Courtesy of Historical
Society of the Tonawandas.*

ings, which made up parts of three villages, and it submerged seven
miles of highway. This reservoir, too, is of much value for flood
regulation.

As had been planned, the Tonawandas became the western
terminus of the new Barge Canal, and all craft plying between there
and Buffalo had to use the Niagara River and the Black Rock Ship
Canal. From Lockport to Tonawanda, the Barge Canal followed
the Erie Canal channel, except for three short manmade land cuts
between Pendleton and Tonawanda. The cuts formed three islands
in the canalized creek and bypassed three sharp bends. Even

Tonawanda Canal Terminal. Barge Canal craft have been delayed because of heavy ice floes in the Niagara River. Shown here are three steel canal boats, two wooden Erie Canal steamers, one wooden tug, and a number of stave-bowed wooden barges used on the Barge Canal during its early years of operation. Photo *circa* May 1926.

though the bends caused no obstacle to the smaller Erie Canal boats, the canal planners knew that they would hinder the passage of the larger Barge Canal craft. This 10.8-mile section of Tona-wanda Creek was the only natural waterway that was in use on the Erie Canal; it was also the most crooked. I recall that canal drivers made jokes about it; they used to say that the name on the back of the stern boat could be read from the towpath, while rounding some of the bends.

A situation in this Tonawanda Creek area created an excep-tion to the normal height of bridges set by the New York State Legislature. When the Barge Canal was constructed, the route of the New York Central Railroad was changed going through the

Tonawandas, and it was obliged to build a new railroad bridge at the eastern end of the long canal terminals in the two cities. Against its protest, the railroad company was compelled to construct an expensive jackknife-type lift bridge with unlimited passageway and clearance. The bridge had more than the normal, 15½-foot clearance above the water; and, during its existence, it has been raised only a few times for testing purposes. The bascule or swing bridge in the Tonawandas also allows unlimited clearance. The reason for these two "exceptions" was a legislative amendment in 1910; bridges over the canalized Tonawanda Creek had to allow for an unobstructed passage for masted vessels, since it was felt essential to terminal development that vessels having masts or funnels be brought in as close as possible for direct transfer of cargo to the canal barges.

I can recall many other engineering features seen on the Barge Canal when it opened, like the different types of dams and the flood gates, and the dimensions of the new channel and the locks, compared to those on the old Erie. Officially, the section that followed the old Erie Canal route across the state was the Erie Division of the New York State Barge Canal System; it used approximately 214 miles of canalized natural waterways and some 126 miles of artificial channels. During the years I was employed on tugs and other craft on the canal, I have been on all its branches and traveled over the Erie Division at least fifty times between Buffalo and Waterford. I came to know by heart all the distances between locks and towns or other points of interest along the canal.

CHAPTER 17

My First Run on the Barge Canal

W HEN the Barge Canal opened on May 15, 1918, I had hired out as a fireman on the tug *Liberty*, a large steam tug which was chartered to the government to tow on the new canal. The wages were based on a monthly scale for a twelve-hour work-day and included board. The Captain received $175 per month, Mate $150, First Engineer $150, and Second Engineer $120. The two firemen and the cook each received $90 per month. The tug operated night and day, and all the crew, except the cook, worked six hours on duty and six hours off.

The employer allowed 90 cents per day, per man, to feed the crew. The Captain received a subsistence check each month and handled what was called the "grub money." It was always suspected that he and the cook split up any surplus money that might be left at the end of the month. Nonetheless, I was usually satisfied with the amount and quality of the food, although there were always some growlers amongst the crew. The growlers were the cause of some of the grub money handlers' acquiring the name of "belly-robber," along with some harsher epithets.

On the tug *Liberty*, the Captain and Mate slept in the after part of the pilot house, in a small, fairly comfortable room containing two bunks. The rest of the seven-man crew slept below decks in the forward end of the tug. The forepeak contained four lower and four upper bunks. It was a fairly comfortable place to sleep in the spring and fall, but it was like an oven in July and

August. Sanitary facilities consisted of only a water closet. Washing up was done in canal water dipped up in a deck pail or hot water drawn from the boiler water supply; a bath was had by the same method. Hot water was plentiful on a steam tug and was also used by most of the crew for hand laundering their own work clothes.

While going through the canal, life took on a monotonous routine. At the end of your six-hour shift, you washed up, ate your meal, sat around for a while, and then went to bed. You were called a half-hour or so before the start of your watch, ate your meal, and then started another six-hour shift. Passing through a town was a welcome break in the mostly rural scenery. Passing through a lock was an interruption of the monotony and provided a half-hour or so of relaxation for the crew and a short rest for the fireman.

For single or footloose men, the life on a canal tug provided just about everything needed except recreation. There were some who found this in a barroom at each end of the canal. For the others, it was work they knew and liked, and it provided the wages needed to support their families. As for me, I enjoyed the work and was contented to work on the canal until I was married in 1928. After that, canal life lost its appeal because of the time that had to be spent away from home and family during the navigation season.

When I hired out as part of the crew, the tug had recently been converted for canal towing, and we stayed in Tonawanda a few days waiting for orders from the canal dispatcher. We used the time to check out things in general and to take aboard needed equipment and other supplies for our first trip over the new canal. There were no canal fleets to tow east, as very few boats had wintered in Buffalo. We finally received orders to proceed to Waterford with the light tug. We ran night and day as far as Lyons, except for the fourteen miles of new canal passing to the south of Rochester. The Barge Canal just about followed the route of the old Erie Canal to the beginning of the canalized Clyde River at Lyons. From here on, we tied up when it became dark, as neither of the pilots was familiar with the canalized rivers used by the new canal, most of the rest of the way to Waterford. In spite of being urged by canal supervisors and dispatchers, there were few if any towboats operated after dark upon the canalized river sections of the new canal, until the pilots made a few trips over the route and became acquainted with the channels.

The route of the Barge Canal follows the general course of the old Erie across New York State. In many places it makes use of the channel of the enlarged Erie. In other parts of the State, it crosses or runs parallel to the old canal. The greatest separation between the old and new canal is about twelve miles—between Syracuse and the Brewerton area at the west end of Oneida Lake.

I recall that on this first trip through the new canal we were all interested in the different scenery and the old landmarks along the route, especially what remained of the old Montezuma aqueduct that used to carry the Erie Canal across the Seneca River, a mile or so west of the village of Montezuma. Some of the stone piers and arches remained on both sides of the river, the center ones having been destroyed and dredged out to make way for the new canalized Seneca River channel. A few of the stone arches are there today, a reminder of the once-busy Erie Canal. Eighteen miles farther on, we passed over the southern end of Cross Lake, which is a small lake about four miles in length. There is an old tradition among the Onondaga Indians respecting an aged and very wise chief who lived on the eastern shore of this lake, several hundred years ago. His name was Hiawatha.

The canalized Seneca River was very crooked as it approached and crossed the lake. Although it was equipped with channel markers or lighted buoys, the pilot had to be observant here, or he found himself going up Cross Lake instead of crossing it.

A mile and three-quarters farther on, we passed under the State Ditch Bridge, which crosses a land cut one-quarter mile long. The cut was dug by the State during Barge Canal construction to bypass a very crooked section of the Seneca River.

Next was Barge Canal Lock 24 at Baldwinsville. This town came to be considered about the halfway point on the new canal. The lock was in the village and there were nearby grocery stores where the tugs and barges replenished food supplies and refilled their drinking water barrels or tanks, while passing through the lock.

The fuel supply was seldom taken aboard at Baldwinsville, for it was usually necessary to fuel up at least twice while towing

Some of the remaining piers and arches of the 800-foot-long aqueduct that carried Erie Canal traffic across the Seneca River. Known as the Richmond or Montezuma Aqueduct, it was a short distance west of the village of Richmond. The other piers were removed at the end of the 1917 canal season to make way for the Barge Canal. Photo *circa* 1923. *Buffalo and Erie County Historical Society.*

through the canal. When the Barge Canal opened, most of the tugs or towboats fueled up with soft coal. A 48 to 60-hour fuel supply was the capacity for most tugs. When fueling up, a part of the supply was stored on deck and was referred to as the deckload. The deckload lasted twenty-four hours or so and was shoveled into the coal bunkers as it was used up. It was a necessary nuisance because it extended the time between fuelings, but made the crewmen scramble around or over it when they went forward or aft.

Pittsford and Rome were the usual fueling stops. For the first season or so the new canal operated, the coal was dumped or piled on the dock, and the tug crewmen were paid fifty cents an hour to shovel it aboard the tug. It being wartime, even the Captain and

Mate pitched in and helped with the fueling. This, however, was a temporary thing, for fueling stations were soon set up along the canal. The coal was then elevated into a storage bin and flowed by gravity aboard the tug.

There was an agent in Baldwinsville who represented the government and some other companies operating on the canal. This man operated a nearby grocery store in the village and could be depended on to supply the passing boats night or day, seven days a week, during the canal season. The tug captains sometimes received orders here, and if it was shortly after the middle or first of the month, the bi-monthly subsistence check and the crews' paychecks might be waiting, along with personal mail sent to the crewmen on the tugs and barges. The supplies put aboard at Baldwinsville usually would last for the rest of the trip.

This village, twelve miles northwest of Syracuse, is named for a doctor, Jonas E. Baldwin, who received the appointment of Physician and Surgeon to the Inland Lock and Navigation Company which was at that time engaged, with several hundred laborers, in constructing the canal and locks at Little Falls. Dr. Baldwin eventually moved to the Township of Lysander in Onondaga County in 1807 and founded the village of Baldwinsville. That same year, for the development of water power, he constructed a dam across the Seneca River. There was a falls at that place and in 1808 he built a canal and lock for the passage of boats around the dam.

In 1839, a towing path was completed on the north bank of the Seneca River, extending from Mud Lock to Baldwinsville, which connected the village with the Erie Canal. In 1850, the State took over the Baldwin's canal, lock, and dam. Shortly thereafter the State extended navigation on the Seneca River for 11¾ miles from Baldwinsville to Jack's Reef. The towing path on this extension was abandoned in 1888.

An interesting anecdote about Dr. Baldwin concerns the year 1816, a memorable one known throughout the country as "the cold year." It is said that frost occurred every month. Crops were injured, the Indians' corn was destroyed, and the Indians were in danger of starvation. Under these circumstances, a deputation of chiefs from the Oneida Nation were sent to Dr. Baldwin (they knowing him to be a man of wealth and benevolence), to request him to furnish them with provisions for the winter. After some inquiries as to their number and necessities, Dr. Baldwin agreed to furnish provisions for one-half the nation. Early in the winter, therefore, they came on, about 250 in number, and encamped in a wood in the vicinity of the village. They remained there until the next spring, drawing their rations daily, like a small army. This well-timed benevolence of Dr. Baldwin saved these destitute people from starvation. The remainder of the nation was fed and carried through the winter by the charity of other individuals.

In the 1840s, an attempt was made to change the name of the village, but the older inhabitants defeated the proposal. They had been eye witnesses to the trials and hardships encountered and endured by Dr. Baldwin and his family. Today, Baldwinsville is an industrious and prosperous village and its name remains as a credit to its founder.

From Baldwinsville, the tug proceeded along the Seneca River, passing by the Syracuse junction branches or sidecuts, then the Cold Spring bridge, and also the Belgium bridge. The next place of interest and early historic background was Three River Point. Here we passed the beginning of the Oswego River on our left and proceeded from the Seneca, up the Oneida River, and went through Lock 23, then to the village of Brewerton, located at the west end of Oneida Lake.

The village is at or near the site of old Fort Brewerton, which was erected by the British in 1759 to protect the Western Frontier against the incursions of the French and their Indian allies. Named for Captain George Brewerton, Jr., an officer in the British army, Fort Brewerton was abandoned by the British and burned by the Indians in 1767.

By 1794 the Indians had become so troublesome that an early settler at Brewerton was granted permission by Governor George Clinton to erect a blockhouse near the site of the old fort. Oliver Stevens kept what was called a "boatmen's tavern," furnishing provisions and other necessaries to those who passed that way. Although the blockhouse was erected for the protection of the nearby settlers, it also must have protected the crewmen and their batteau cargoes from Indian raiding parties. Many of these craft must have been delayed here when traveling eastward by adverse lake conditions, for Brewerton was on the avenue of commerce

A former Erie Canal steamer westbound on the Oneida River with a tow of empty Barge Canal boats. Photo *circa* 1925. *Buffalo and Erie County Historical Society.*

used by the early traders and trappers traveling to and from Schenectady and Albany before the opening of the Erie Canal.

On this first trip in 1918, we passed Brewerton on a nice spring day, and the run across Oneida Lake was made in a little over two hours with the light tug. We left Sylvan Beach behind and then passed through Locks 22 and 21. They are the same locks for which we unloaded gravel at the hamlet of Grove Springs. The hamlet is no longer there, having been absorbed by Stacey's Basin after the closing of the Erie Canal. The run from here was over an artificial or man-made canal to Frankfort, where we entered the canalized Mohawk River.

The next point of interest was the lock at Little Falls. This lock replaced four Erie Canal locks and has a 40.5-foot drop, and a lift gate at its lower end instead of swinging gates. The eight bridge dams at the locks along the Mohawk were something new and interesting to the crew as they were the first dams of this type that we had ever seen. At this time, an old wooden suspension bridge spanned the Mohawk River at the foot of Lock 12 from Tribes Hill to Fort Hunter.

At Schenectady, some of the spans and piers of a very old and odd-looking covered wooden bridge were still to be seen in the Mohawk, the center part of the bridge and piers having been removed for Barge Canal navigation. A little farther along the Mohawk, at Rexford Flats, we passed between the remaining piers of the old 610-foot-long Erie Canal upper aqueduct. After leaving Rexford, the river kept widening out, and we next passed through Lock 7 at Visher's Ferry with its 27-foot-high, very wide fixed dam. Then 12.7 miles from the upper aqueduct we went between the remaining piers of the longest aqueduct on the old Erie. This 1,137-foot span crossed the Mohawk at the village of Crescent.

A mile or so farther on, we entered a land cut that contained two guard gates and five new locks which are sometimes referred to as the Waterford Flight. This flight replaced the 16 Erie Canal locks on the south side of the Mohawk at Cohoes. The greatest distance between the locks is about 0.6 mile between Locks 3 and 4. The other locks are spaced about a quarter-mile apart. When descending the Waterford Flight from the Mohawk to the Hudson Valley, boaters had a view that reminds one of a giant set of stairs.

My first trip with the light tug *Liberty* over the new canal had been uneventful, but it was nevertheless very interesting. We had arrived at Waterford four days after leaving Tonawanda; had we not tied up at dark, we would have made it in three.

We laid idle in Waterford seven or eight days waiting for our tow of boats to arrive from New York City in a Hudson River tow. While waiting, all of the crew were getting a full night's sleep, and we were quite content to be fed and paid for loafing. As firemen, my partner or I banked the fire at night, and if the engineers so ordered, we let the steam rise in the boiler in the daytime.

I recollect that my partner's and my loafing was interrupted by having to replenish the tug's drinking and cooking water supply. There being no freshwater tap or outlet on the terminal, we had to do it with pails by walking with one in each hand to a water tap half a block from the tug. We must have made fifteen trips each to fill the water storage container aboard that tug! I ought to have mentioned it before, but large tugs from the Buffalo area carried no deckhands, and, although I was hired as a fireman, I had to handle towlines and tie-up lines, and take care of other duties that were usually handled by a deckhand. Later on, the larger Barge Canal tugs carried two deckhands as well as the two firemen.

Under the fireman-deckhand arrangement, we were at the beck and call of the Captain, the Mate, and the engineers. So, to keep us from getting too soft and lazy while waiting for our tow, they had us scrub the inside of the pilot house and engine room. This we did, while the Powers That Be did their heavy thinking.

Our layover at Waterford soon ended, and we returned to Buffalo with a tow of empty grain boats. This was the first of many trips that I made over the Barge Canal from 1918 to 1935.

CHAPTER 18

The Barge Canal
Under Government Operation

IN THE SPRING of 1919, I did not go back on the *Liberty*, which was still working for the government. I went to work that spring as a fireman-deckhand on the small wooden tug *Wm. G. Fox*, also owned by the Cowles Towing Company, which had contracted to tow, from Buffalo to New York City, four empty covered or housed-over wooden barges owned by the Erie Railroad. The four empty scows made a long tow, and two tugs were used to take the tow through the Barge Canal. The *Merchant*, a rather large, steel, steam tug, did the towing; and I was on the small stern tug that tailed or guided the end of the tow. Both tugs were single crewed, and we ran twelve hours a day going through the canal.

A makeshift kitchen or galley had been set up inside one of the covered barges, and a cook had been employed to feed both tug crews and the four-man barge crew. We had breakfast before starting out in the morning, stopped the tow at lunch time, and ate again after we tied up in the evening. The cook had only a black, iron wood-burning cook stove in his makeshift kitchen, and had eleven people and himself for whom to cook and wash dishes. The cook became rather cranky because of over-work, for when we were about halfway through the canal, in the cook's presence, one of the barge men made a jovial remark about the homemade pie we did *not* have for supper. The cook gave him a dirty look and ignored him. But a day or so later the same thing happened, and the cook blew up and threatened to stick a butcher knife into the fellow. The bargeman was so unnerved by the threat that he quit the tow that evening and went home.

We continued on through the canal without further incident, and when we arrived at Crescent we stopped at the canal terminal for a half hour to unload some furniture from one of the covered barges that Mr. Cowles had shipped to a relative who lived in the village. We then continued on with the tow, tailing it as far as the government lock at Troy. The tug *Merchant* then continued on to New York with the four barges.

We began our return trip to Buffalo with the light tug. We had to feed ourselves on the trip home, for the cook had been paid off, the galley equipment was stored aboard, and the cook stove was set up on the open stern deck of our small tug—there was no room to put it inside.

We started back to Buffalo with two lengths of stove pipe rising up from the cook stove on the stern deck and with a steam hose connected to a 3-inch portable siphon which was placed in the bilge through a hatch between the wooden tow bits. The tug's regular siphon was too small to keep the bilges free of water when the tug was running light, for it squatted down and water poured in through the dry seams under the stern fantail. We made it back to Buffalo all right with our rather ludicrous looking craft, which caused many an amused glance on the way. Here we removed the siphon and got rid of the cook stove.

We did some short towing in the Buffalo area, but I was out of work for a while in that summer of 1919. When I heard that a second engineer was needed on the former ferry tug, *Wm. D. Kropp,* which was laying at the canal terminal in North Tonawanda, I applied for the job. I was sixteen years old, and no license was required by a second engineer at that time. The Chief Engineer looked at me rather askance because of my age, but I got the job because there were few qualified men available.

The *Kropp* was a medium-size tug, and the crew consisted of a Captain and Mate, two engineers (who also fired the boiler themselves), one deck hand, and a cook. My wages were $120 per month and board.

A number of unusual incidents happened that season while I was on the *Kropp.* I believe it was because the new government

New concrete barge *U.S. 107* tied up at the Ellicott Creek Boatyard at Tonawanda, N.Y., in midsummer of 1919. Scaffold hanging from port bow indicates the boat was there for repairs. Diagonal pieces of wood fastened along
the side were a type of wooden fender used to prevent damage to the boat's
sides while in transit.

fleet of barges came on the canal that year. They were built especially for the Barge Canal and consisted of 51 steel barges 150
feet long by 20 feet wide, 12 feet deep, of 630 tons cargo capacity
each. Twenty-one concrete barges 150 feet long by 21 feet wide,
12 feet deep, cargo capacity 520 tons each, and three wooden
barges of the same general dimensions were operated.

The concrete barges were conceived and built during World
War I. It was hoped that they would be a workable substitute for
steel, which had a high priority because of the war. However, the
barges made such a poor showing on the canal that the Munson

Steamship Company declined to take them over when it bought the fleet after the government ceased operating the New York State Barge Canal.

The concrete barges were not much of a success commercially or otherwise. They drew 4 feet of water when empty compared to a wooden or steel barge's 18 to 22 inches. The sides were 4 inches thick, of heavily reinforced concrete, but they were easily holed and sunk when they struck a solid object with a moderate force that would not have damaged a steel or wooden barge. And many of them were damaged or sunk along the canal between Albany and Buffalo. To the best of my knowledge, none of them had a useful life of more than three or four years.

Some of the concrete barges that were not sunk and destroyed ended up as bulkheads or were used to lengthen short approach walls on some of the locks along the Mohawk River. Two of them are part of a landfill in the old Erie Canal bed at the foot of Henry Street in Buffalo. They are buried there today under the Niagara section of the New York State Thruway.

Contracts for twenty-five concrete barges were let to four companies by the Inland Waterways Committee of the Railroad Administration (which operated the Barge Canal for the federal government during the war). The pouring of concrete for the first Tonawanda-built barges was started on November 15, 1918; they were launched, completed, and put into service in the summer of 1919. The cost was $25,000 each. A unique method of building and launching the concrete barges was devised by the builders at the boatyard property adjacent to Ellicott Creek. A 4½-foot deep basin capable of holding the barges had been dug out and the barges were built in the dry excavation. When the barges were completed, a channel was dug from the basin to Ellicott Creek. The basin was then filled with water and the four barges were floated into Ellicott Creek, which led into the Barge Canal.

When I hired out on the *Kropp*, we spent two weeks waiting in the Tonawandas for a tow to take down the canal. While there, we were given orders to tow two of the new concrete boats from the yard on Ellicott Creek where five of them had been built. We towed them out to the canal terminal, and a larger tug towed them to Buffalo the next day where they finished fitting out and loaded grain for the Atlantic Seaboard.

A steel steam towboat and three steel barges, right, designed to fill a Barge Canal lock. The boats were built as a wartime emergency fleet by the United States government, but World War I was over before they appeared on the new Barge Canal. Because of a railroad car shortage the boats were put to good use hauling grain and other commodities to the eastern seaboard for Europe in the postwar period. *Buffalo and Erie County Historical Society.*

Then after waiting a few more days, we hooked on to three of the new steel barges loaded with grain and started down the canal for Waterford. The steel barges were designed for easy towing, but they did not handle well on a long towline. They dove all over the canal when towed at a normal speed, and were hard to manage and keep in the channel because of their design. The steel barges gained a reputation for doing a lot of damage along the canal. Many of them soon appeared with large dents and caved-in bows. I saw steel lampposts that had been knocked down by the overhanging, sloped bows when the boats rode up on the lock wall while attempting to enter the lock. On canal wag said that the farmers along the crooked part of the level above Baldwinsville put their cows in the barn when they heard that a tow of these steel boats was coming, because one of the fleets had run up into a pasture and killed some cows. They became easier to handle later on

when a concrete or wooden barge was put in a tow with two of
the steel barges.

We got as far as Rochester with our tow of these three barges
without any trouble, arriving there about 3 A.M. There was some
current in the Genesee River which crossed the canal here, but the
Captain didn't believe it was strong enough to bother our tow. We
started across, had to pull upstream to hold the boats against the
current, and were able to enter the canal on the east side of the
river with the tug and the tow without mishap. But when the stern
of our tow got out into the current, it was carried downstream and
we were unable to keep the front end of our three-boat tow from
striking a concrete arch-type bridge that was under construction
on the east side of the river, a short distance from the crossing. No
concrete had been poured, but the wooden forms and reinforcing
iron were in place ready for the concrete. The tug passed under
the bridge, but the head boat struck the supports for the bridge
forms and the whole thing came crashing down, landing partly on
the bow of the head boat. There was so much wood and tangled
reinforcing rods lying on the bow of the head boat that the tug
had to tie a line to it and pull it clear before we could go on with
the tow.

Had the tug and tow been privately owned, it would have
meant a big damage suit. As it was, the tug captains made out a
report to the government canal authorities, and we heard no more
of the matter. We finished that trip to Waterford with no more
trouble.

A mishap occurred later that summer as we entered Lock 29
at Palmyra. We were towing three light concrete barges back to
Buffalo at the time. The first two were towed abreast of each
other, and the bargemen had failed to keep the breast lines tight.
This allowed the boats to spread apart so that a hole was punched
in each of them when entering the lock. Fortunately, the damage
was above the waterline of both barges and they were repaired at
Buffalo.

Another well-remembered incident took place that fall which
happened while towing eastbound one wooden and two concrete
barges loaded with grain. I was still on the tug *Kropp* and we had
left Buffalo and arrived at Baldwinsville about four days later with
the three barges. After taking aboard our groceries and other sup-

A group of Barge Canal fleets at Brewerton, N.Y., in the winter of 1936-37. The eastbound fleets were stopped here because of ice conditions farther along the canal.

plies, we were delayed about three or four hours because the wife of the barge Captain on the stern concrete barge had delivered a baby while we waited tied up below the lock. All went well with the new arrival, and we left Baldwinsville late that afternoon with the mother and new baby aboard the last barge.

Arriving at Brewerton early the next morning, we started across Oneida Lake, which was calm at the time. During the day, the wind began to pick up, and by the time we neared Sylvan Beach late that afternoon, it was blowing hard from dead astern. We had no trouble with the tow in the lake, but we had to change our course to enter between the breakwall piers at Sylvan Beach. This put the tug and the tow in the trough of the seas. We could all see that we were in for trouble, since the wind by this time was blowing about 35 miles an hour. The Chief Engineer had taken over in the engine room while I stayed below and fired the boiler. The wind was strong enough to blow down our smoke stack, a hinged and counter-weighted affair that could be lowered by hand to allow the tug to pass under low bridges. I had to go out on the deck, which was awash, to raise the stack back in place. While doing so, the seas washed in through the open boiler room door and from then until we got inside, I was standing in three or four inches of water sloshing around on the firehold floor during our entrance to the harbor. The tug, a concrete barge, and a wooden barge managed to get in the harbor, although the concrete barge hit the breakwater wall and knocked a hole in its bow ahead of the watertight bulkhead between the cargo hold and the bow compartment. The bow settled down for a foot or so when this compartment filled with water, but no damage was done to the cargo. The wooden middle boat was not damaged, but the other concrete or stern barge broke loose from the tow outside of the breakwater and drifted on to the sandy beach on the Verona side of the breakwater piers.

After we got inside the harbor, we could see the barge lying on the beach with the seas breaking over its full length. The barge Captain, his wife, and the day-old baby were safely inside the cabin. That evening after the wind had gone down, a small boat brought the Captain and his family ashore from the beached barge, seemingly none the worse for their experience on the lake.

The next day, with the help of some other tugs, we pulled the beached barge into deep water. It had sustained no damage, and we brought it into the harbor. We stayed at Sylvan Beach for a couple of days while the damaged concrete barge was patched and pumped out; the damaged rigging was repaired, and we then proceeded without further trouble to Waterford.

We made one more round trip that fall, and when we arrived at Waterford with three steel barges, we were given orders to deliver them to New York. We stayed in Waterford the next day because a heavy rainstorm up north had caused high water and a fast current in the upper Hudson River. That evening, the steamer *Witherbee*, with three loaded iron ore barges, arrived from up north at the Troy lock. The fast current caused one of the barges to break loose from the tow while entering the lock, and it drifted over and hung up on the lock dam. It was thought urgent to get the barge off the dam while the water was still high, so the tug *Latimore*, which lay near us that evening, was given orders to attempt it. The crew was not to be found, and the Chief and I went over on the tug as part of the crew. When we arrived at the dam, I did not think we would be able to do anything because of the high water and fast current. I did not reason that the tug could go any place the loaded barge could drift. So we were able to put a tow line aboard the barge, and with the help of the *Witherbee*, we were able to pull the undamaged barge away from the dam. As far as I can remember, that was a thank-you rescue job. The next day, the water and current had subsided enough for us to start our trip down the Hudson with the government fleet.

The trip to New York was made without incident, and when we arrived there, I was paid off and given my railroad fare to Buffalo, so I went home. The tug wintered in New York and I can't recall if the government used it on the canal the next year or not.

The government-built towboats were in operation the following season, 1920, on the Barge Canal. However, in the spring, I went to work for Cowles on a medium-size steam tug and spent a couple of months towing some Erie Canal-size boats carrying paving stone from Hulberton to Buffalo. When the job was finished, I hired out as a deckhand on the new government canal steamer *Saratoga* and, after a few days' layover, we hooked onto three steel barges and towed them to Waterford.

A rather somber and well-remembered incident took place there aboard the *Saratoga*. We were tied up between Locks 2 and 3 as there was no room at the canal terminal below Lock 2. That evening, Captain Jack Saunders, a man of about fifty, who made his home in Buffalo, was reading while lying in his bunk with the stateroom door open. In a short time, one of the crewmen noticed that he was gasping for breath. I and some others went into the stateroom to see if we could help him, but he soon became unconscious. A doctor was called and soon after his arrival, the Captain was pronounced dead from what turned out to be a heart attack. I was part of the group that carried the body ashore that evening. I was only seventeen at the time, and whenever I passed the pilot house in the dark afterwards, I got a spooky feeling because of the Captain's sudden demise. I had worked with him before in Buffalo.

Life goes on, for the next day a new Captain came aboard and we soon started back for Buffalo with another tow of three steel barges. All went well until we arrived at Cross Lake on the Seneca River, west of Baldwinsville. It was daylight early in the morning, but rather foggy. The skipper lost sight of the channel

The Buffalo Drydock, July 1920, was a graving dock that filled with water by gravity and was emptied by large electric pumps. The brand-new steamer *Saratoga* was built for the Barge Canal. The excursion steamer at the rear is the *Ossian Bedell* that carried passengers between Buffalo and Fort Erie Beach. The lake steamer in the background is unloading package freight at the mile-long freight house on Ohio Street. The drydock and freight house are gone, as are the vessels in the picture. *Buffalo and Erie County Historical Society.*

markers and we headed north on Cross Lake instead of crossing it. When the fog suddenly lifted, our location was noticed, and we returned to the west entrance of the river without going aground. It was a hectic incident for a short time which, fortunately, did not involve any damage.

The *Saratoga* and all the government-built steam-powered tow boats were oil burners. They burned thick, heavy, black crude oil and it was stored in built-in twin tanks under the stern deck. Soon after leaving Cross Lake behind, the engineers began having trouble with the fuel oil supply, which could only be pumped from the starboard fuel tank. The steamer began to list to port, the fuel was getting low in the starboard tank, and we were in danger of running out of fuel. So the other deckhand and I were put to work transferring oil from one tank to the other, with deck pails (a piece of rope tied to a pail). The engineers finally corrected the trouble, and we arrived in Buffalo in November.

It was near the middle of the month by the time the fleet was loaded with grain for the Seaboard. I decided then that I would not make the last trip down the canal, for I knew that I would be paid off at the end of the trip in Albany or New York and have to come home on the train. Thinking of the recent fuel oil transfer job also helped to make up my mind. I got off in Tonawanda, in the fall of 1920, which was the last year of Barge Canal control and operation by the government.

The Munson Steamship Company with its headquarters in New York City bought the government Barge Canal fleet. It became known on the canal as the "Green Fleet" because of its color. The steamers and barges were just as unmanageable under the Munson Company as they were under government operations. Different methods of towing them were tried, but they were not adaptable to the restricted structures and waterways of the Barge Canal. In the spring of 1926 the Munson Company began an Express Packet freight service between Albany and Buffalo with two of its steamers—the *Ontario* and *Monroe,* I believe. The service was of short duration, and I was told that the "Green Fleet" finally wound up in Cuba.

CHAPTER 19

The Erie and Champlain Canals

I MENTIONED before that there were but a few tugs of suitable size available for use on the Barge Canal when it first opened. By 1921 the Cowles Towing Company had purchased four idle Lake Erie fish tugs—idle because the fishing industry had petered out. The tugs, built of wood and well past their prime, had been converted to canal tugs and were all used in service on the canal until the Depression of the 1930s came along. The tugs were of medium size, and I spent part of that season of 1921 as second engineer on one of them doing my own firing. It was hard work, especially in the hot weather, as we worked six hours on and six off. We were towing from Buffalo to Waterford. Each time we arrived at Buffalo the Chief Engineer, an elderly man, went ashore, and when it was about time to depart, came aboard drunk. He immediately went to bed and left it up to me to keep the tug running for the next ten hours or so or until he recovered from his hangover. I could only get a couple of hours sleep before going back on watch again. After this happened a couple of times, I quit and spent the rest of the season working on a Tonawanda-owned tug as second engineer. The tug had been chartered for the season to tow four deck barges carrying structural steel between Buffalo and Troy.

In 1922 I worked ashore for a time until being laid off. While out of work I saw the Erie Canal steamer *Red Jacket* with its push boat and four-boat tow lying at the canal terminal in Tonawanda

taking on supplies. Since they were short handed, I hired out for
$80 a month and board as deckhand on the tow. I was too young
and light to do any steering. We were towed on a long hawser and
had a good trip through the canal and down the Hudson River.
When we arrived in New York, I was fired because I had refused to
cut firewood for the cook on the steamer. I was paid off and hung
around the waterfront until evening and then took the night boat
to Albany. The fare, including a stateroom, I recall, was $6. Arriv-
ing at Albany the next morning, I had breakfast ashore and then
took a bus to Waterford, hoping to find a job on a fleet going east
or west.

I arrived at the terminal there about the same time that another steam canal boat pulled in with a tow of five light grain
boats (Erie Canal size). This was the type of steamer that had
come on the Erie Canal in the 1870s; such steamers were still in
use on the Barge Canal until the early 1930s. The one that arrived
at Waterford when I did was the *James W. Follette,* built in Tonawanda about 1912 and still in good operating condition. The
Follette was short a second engineer and I took the job, at $90 per
month and board. I had seen many steam canal boats during my
canal days, but this was the first one I ever worked on. They
carried a five-man crew—a Captain and Mate, two engineers, and a
deckhand. The crew ate in the main cabin, which was also the
Captain's family living quarters. The Mate slept on the push boat;
the two engineers and the deckhand slept below decks in a bunk
room or bow compartment on the forward end of the steamer.

The *Follette* was powered by a single expansion engine built
by the Hall Engine and Machine Company in Lockport. A surface
condenser was also a part of the power plant which made it economical for the steamer to operate in fresh or salt water. They were
cleaner and easier to fire and were smokeless because they burned
hard instead of soft coal. Although the wages were $30 lower than
those paid on a tug, the working conditions and the accommodations were much better except for one thing: I did not like the
sleeping quarters. I have never forgotten that one morning after I
came off watch I was lying in my bottom bunk just about to doze
off, when I felt something run across my bare feet, sticking out
from under the covers. I was startled awake in time to see a rat
running across the bunkroom floor. I was a long time getting to

sleep after that unnerving incident. I came awake with a start another time when I thought I felt something furry brush my cheek while lying in my bunk but did not see anything that might have caused it. You can believe that I changed from the bottom to an upper bunk at the first opportunity. The steam canal boats going east usually carried grain as part of their cargo. This caused them to become infested with rats, which I saw scurrying about the floor of the cargo hold when the steamer's grain cargo was being cleaned up during the unloading. Rats are poor bedfellows, but are good sailors and can be found on any vessel where food is available.

In spite of my dislike for those mostly unseen passengers, I made three round trips on the *Follette* and received my final paycheck in New York that fall and came home on the train.

In 1923, I went firing on a large wooden tug named *The Rochester* and, after being on this tug for a few weeks, the second engineer quit and I was given the second's job. The tug was towing for a new firm, The Rochester Terminal and Transportation Company, which had built its own receiving and loading station in the rock cut a short distance west of the Genesee River. Although their boats brought some commodities west, most of the freight consisted of salt that was loaded at Rochester and shipped east. We also made two trips that summer to Watkins Glen at the south end of Seneca Lake, where our tow loaded salt at the docks of the International Salt Company for shipment eastward. I had not been up beyond Waterloo since I was a young lad in 1915. I enjoyed the scenery, as my last trip up that way had been on the old Cayuga-Seneca Canal on my father's canal boats. On our second trip, while waiting for the boats to load, I found time to enjoy a walking tour of the well-known Watkins Glen.

By 1923, the Rochester Terminal and Transportation Company had purchased tugs of its own, and The Cowles Towing Company's tug *Rochester* was towing tank barges for the Standard Oil Company. That spring I went to work for a Tonawanda tug owner as second engineer. The tug was chartered to tow four wooden deck barges carrying reinforcing and structural steel between Buffalo and Troy. We made two round trips when the job ended and I was laid off in midsummer.

It seemed that I always could rely on Mr. Cowles for a job, so

I got in touch with him. In a few days he called me and said he had an engineer's job open. I said I would take it and was sent to the city of Rochester where I boarded the tug which was furnishing steam to pump out its tow of two gasoline barges at the Standard Oil Company dock in the rock cut west of the Genesee. During that summer we towed the same two barges and always waited for them to load at Albany. We also delivered gasoline to Utica, Rome, and Syracuse as well as Rochester, which was as far west as we got for the rest of the three and a half months of that season. During that summer, neither I nor the other engineer had a Federal Marine License and, at that time, as far as I know, the canal was under State control and none was required. It was getting near fall when the Captain received a telephone call at one of the locks as we were returning to Albany. The call was from the tug's owner, Mr. Cowles, who told the Captain that the tug was scheduled to make a trip with two barge loads of kerosene to be delivered to a number of ports on Lake Champlain, which was Federal waters; any steam vessels operating on the lake required licensed officers. Mr. Cowles suggested to the Captain that I should go before the United States Steamboat Inspectors at Albany and take an examination for a Chief Engineer's License. I had been preparing for the examination but did not intend to take it until the next year. However, when we arrived at Waterford, the tug proceeded with the two empty barges to Albany to load kerosene, while I took a bus from there to the Steamboat Inspector's office. Late that afternoon I finished the examination and was presented with a Chief Engineer's License, which I accepted with a feeling of accomplishment, for I had been studying for that moment for three years.

I knew that our tow of barges would start loading as soon as they arrived at Albany and would probably already be on their way north, so I telephoned the Troy lock from the Inspector's office and learned that the tug and two barges had gone through there an hour ago. The locktender suggested that I take a bus to Mechanicville and meet the boats at a nearby lock. By late that afternoon I was back onboard, on the way up the Champlain Canal to Whitehall, where we took aboard a Lake Champlain pilot and then continued through the Lake Champlain Narrows and into the lake. Although double crewed, we only ran daylight hours when going from place to place on the lake. The pilot was a Frenchman very familiar with these waters, and I recall that the first evening we tied up overnight was at a place which he called Snakes Den. The place was a deep-water, forested cove that I think was used as an emergency shelter under stormy lake conditions. The next day, as we continued northward, we discharged portions of the barges' cargo at Ticonderoga, Crown Point, Port Henry, and Rouses' Point, where we stayed overnight. It was Prohibition time, and Rouses' Point being near the Canadian Border, Black Horse ale was in good supply. That evening, the Captain and the other engineer went ashore and took on a cargo of ale. When they returned to the tug that night they were literally poured aboard the tug by the crew so that they would not fall into the lake. From Rouses' Point, the last stop on the New York side of the lake, we went to Burlington, Vermont, where we discharged the balance of the kerosene cargo before returning to Albany with the light barges. It was the last trip of the season and a good one, as we had encountered no mishaps or bad weather while on Lake Champlain. It had been my first trip to that area over the Barge Canal. After three and a half months' absence, I was a little bit homesick and glad to get back to Buffalo, even though it meant being laid off. One of the first things I did that fall was to have my new license framed to hang in my bedroom, where it was proudly displayed through the winter months.

That winter of 1923, I took a job in a local paper mill; the eight-hour law had not yet gone into effect, and I worked two shifts of eleven hours when on days, and thirteen hours when on nights. I kind of liked the work and even got a small promotion, but did not relish working inside in the summertime.

About June 1, 1924, I quit the paper mill and went to work as a coal-passer on a Great Lakes wooden lumber steamer, or "hooker," as they were called then. The steamer, owned by the North Tonawanda Lumber Company, delivered lumber to the company's docks from upper lake ports. My duties as a coal-passer were to keep the fireman supplied with fuel from the ship's coal storage space or coal bunkers. I also helped him to clean fires, and I disposed of the ashes after the fires were cleaned. There were two coal-passers and we worked six hours on and six off.

We left North Tonawanda with the light steamer for Lake

This type of steamer brought lumber from upper Great Lakes ports to the Tonawandas when they were busy lumber ports in the late nineteenth and early twentieth centuries. They became known as lumber hookers, because they sometimes hooked onto and towed as many as three schooner-type lumber barges on the lakes.

Huron, where we were to load rough sawed white pine lumber at a place called Sprague, a small port on Georgian Bay in Canada. In the early 1900s, when Tonawanda was still a busy lumber port, I had seen these small wooden steamers arrive at Tonawanda with two loaded lumber barges in tow. On this trip we had no tow, for the lumber business was fading out. Loading required four days, and the ship's deckhands were paid extra for handling lumber while we were loading. The rest of the crew loafed around most of the time, now and then playing poker. I won $35 on the trip, which amounted to more than the $30 wages I drew at the end of the two-week voyage.

The food and sleeping quarters were good. The coal-passers had a stateroom containing an upper and lower bunk to themselves. I lost my liking for the sleeping quarters when I was awakened one night from scratching myself. When I turned on the light, I found that once again I had bedfellows; this time it was bedbugs. These insects were common on the old wooden vessels at that time. I made only the one trip on a Great Lakes vessel, for it did not appeal to me, so I finished the season working on Barge Canal tugs.

More and more, I preferred working for a Buffalo-based company so that I could visit home frequently during the canalling season. Then, at the end of the 1928 season I married a local girl and established our home in Tonawanda. That made getting home throughout the season even more important. In this situation, too, there were fewer job opportunities for me in the 1930s, since most of the tugs operating on the canal were from the eastern end of the State.

Like everything else, constant changes had taken place on the canal over the years. Starting back in 1921, other transportation companies began operating on the canal with more modern equipment which included new and larger barges and more powerful tugs. That same season, the Standard Oil Company introduced five new self-propelled tankers on the canal, which carried petroleum products to tank depots it had built along the canal between Buffalo and Albany. Other companies built vessels designed for combined canal and lake service. One company built five motor vessels that could load grain at Duluth and deliver it to the Atlantic Seaboard via the Great Lakes, Barge Canal, and the Hudson River.

At one time or another, every conceivable kind of freight was shipped over the Barge Canal. An unusual but interesting instance of perishable freight was a cargo of live eels. The shipment, originating at Quebec, was carried in four specially constructed barges which entered the canal at Oswego, and it was speedily transported to the New York market. Barge loads of other perishable commodities like potatoes, apples, and onions were such that the development of a refrigerator barge was considered. Even automobile shipments, which started because of a railroad car shortage, became common on the canal.

Out of the port of Buffalo in 1924 by way of the Barge Canal, 23,462,920 bushels of various kinds of grain floated to the Atlantic Seaboard. As time went on, the shipping trends changed

The foreground shows a section of the old Erie Canal in Buffalo, which was filled in (1935) and is now a part of the Niagara section of the Thruway. Middle ground is a section of the Black Rock Ship Canal and retaining wall. The background shows the beginning of the Niagara River. Photo 1932.

on the canal and the preponderance of freight moved westward. Molasses, sugar, flaxseed, and petroleum products came into Buffalo by way of the canal. Large quantities of phosphate rock, nitrate of soda, and sulphur were shipped to Trenton, Ontario, from the East.

When completed, the Barge Canal System was estimated to be able to handle 20,000,000 tons of cargo per year, but the nearest approach to that figure was 5,015,206 tons in 1936; thereafter, the tonnages began to fall each year until in 1957 it was down to 2,675,853 tons. In 1959, the new St. Lawrence Seaway route opened, and tonnages have continued to drop until now the Barge Canal handles little else but petroleum products shipped by tank barges propelled by pusher tugs.

CHAPTER 20

Tug Engineer

I BEGAN WORKING for Benjamin L. Cowles at the age of thirteen, becoming fourteen in August 1917. I never returned to school. I worked on and off for Cowles in different kinds of jobs until the end of 1924. In the spring of 1925, I began working steady each season for Cowles as Chief Engineer on the steam tug *Liberty*, towing on the Barge Canal. In 1927 I began working year 'round on a Cowles-owned tug towing a grain barge twice a week, all through the winter in Buffalo Harbor. Between trips I did maintenance and repair work on the tugs wintering at his small shipyard in Buffalo.

Mr. Cowles died in 1930, and his wife carried on the business until the end of 1934. She sold all the tugs and the shipyard, and I was out of a job in the middle of the Depression. At that time, I had been married for six years and had two small daughters and a $3,000 mortgage on a house that we had moved into in 1930.

I laid around that winter until mid-January when I got a job, starting at 35 cents an hour, in a local plant that manufactured raw materials for the plastics industry. Although I was offered a foreman's job in the plastics plant in March, I decided not to take it. I had contracted an itch from the chemical dust and quit the first of April to take a job as engineer on a Lake Erie fish-tug at Dunkirk, New York.

The fishing season lasted about six weeks when the whitefish, pike, and perch were running, and in earlier years I had heard tug

A pair of partly loaded Erie Canal boats passing the Erie County Penitentiary between Pennsylvania and Hudson Streets, Buffalo, N.Y. Two towlines on the bow of the head boat indicate two teams on the towpath. The penitentiary was abandoned and replaced by another in a rural section of Erie County in the 1920s. Photo *circa* early 1900s. *Buffalo and Erie County Historical Society.*

engineers tell of making $200 a week when the fishing was good. At that time they received $5 per day and a percentage share of the catch. By the time I hired out the fishing had fallen off, and the fish-tug owners were only percentage paying on the catch; no wages were paid to the five-man crew. I took the job, hoping that it would be a good season, and went to Dunkirk by myself, boarding with some friends of mine at $10 a week.

That spring of 1935, due no doubt to an upset in the ecology of Lake Erie, few whitefish were to be caught. When the gillnets were hauled, they were covered with a type of algae the fishermen called "green slime," and they predicted a poor fishing season. At the end of three weeks we had caught only a thousand pounds of whitefish and my share came to twenty dollars. I was out one week's board, so I quit and went home.

About May 1, 1935, I went to work as Chief Engineer on the wooden canal steam-tug *C. F. Coughlin.* William Murphy, the Captain-owner of the tug, was a man I had known since I was a young boy on my father's canal boats, hauling gravel from Palmyra. Murph, or Will, as he was called when spoken to, was a big, easy-going six-footer. He always wore a moustache because he had a harelip, and he spoke in a nasal tone of voice. Though known and referred to as "Harelip Murphy" because of his impediment, he was never addressed that way because of his size. He was usually a cheerful sort of a fellow, and I always liked him. I recall that when he got into a friendly argument he always ended his part of the discussion with the flat statement "No argument."

In the Palmyra days when I first knew him, Murph was mate on the small wooden steam-tug *E. W. Sutton,* which towed our Erie Canal boats during the years that we boated gravel for Barge Canal construction. The *E. W. Sutton* was a former Lake Erie fish-tug converted for canal towing. The Captain's sleeping quarters were in the rear of the pilot house. A kitchen or galley, as it was always called on tugs, was added on the stern deck, and the rest of the five-man crew slept below decks in the forward end of the tug. I knew and called all of the crew by their first names. Edward Sutton was the Captain and owner of the tug, his brother Dave was Chief Engineer, the Captain's son Edward was second engineer and, of course, Will Murphy was the Mate. There was also a combination cook-deckhand who hailed from Grand Island; the rest of the crew lived in Buffalo.

The Captain was paralyzed from the waist down, and got around on a rather high stool with four casters on it. He never left the pilot house in which he made his toilette, and his meals were served to him there. When the tug and tow was under way the Captain wheeled or steered the tug all day and Murph did all the night-time steering. In spite of his affliction, Captain Sutton was good-natured and Murph waited on him hand and foot. The family name of Sutton was well-known in marine circles in the early 1900s. They were marine steam-engine designers and builders, and their name appeared on many tugboat steam engines. Will Murphy was the only one of the crew of the tug *Sutton* that I came in contact with after we finished boating gravel at the end of 1915.

About the spring of 1921, when I worked as second engineer

on one of Cowles' tugs, Will Murphy was the Captain. His wife, a short, pleasant woman, was the cook. The wooden tug had been a Lake Erie fish tug named the *Seawing;* renamed the *Loraine,* it was towing canal fleets between Buffalo and Waterford. This was the only tug I ever worked on that had a woman cook. The Captain slept in the pilot house and the rest of the crew slept below decks in the forward end of the tug, except for the cook. Special arrangements were made for her to sleep in the small six-foot-wide by eight-foot-long galley. A bunk three feet wide was hinged to the rear wall of the galley. At bedtime the bunk was let down and the cook slept above the table. A curtain drawn across the galley in front of the bunk gave sufficient privacy to dress or undress. The galley could not be closed up in the evening because it was the custom to have coffee on the stove and a lunch set out for the night crew.

Getting back to Murphy and the tug *Coughlin,* there was about two weeks' repair and fit-out work to get the tug ready for the coming season in 1935. This was still Depression time, and it was agreed that I would work for $4 a day getting the tug ready to operate. I would receive $150 a month and board as Chief Engineer when we started towing. Everything worked out as agreed and near the end of May we left Buffalo with a fleet of grain-laden canal barges for Waterford.

There was one thing that made me uneasy about that old wooden tug. No one else mentioned it, but now and then I could smell the odor of charred or smouldering wood. I looked and searched everywhere, but found no sign of fire. I finally reasoned that it must be under the boiler: the timber and planking which supported it must be smouldering. The planking under the boiler of the wooden tug was covered with two or three inches of concrete to insulate it from the hot ashes dropping through the grates; but some of the concrete must have become loose and was hoed out from under the boiler along with the ashes. The bare wood was then exposed to the hot ashes and heat from the firebox grates two feet above the floor. A short time after I had decided what was smouldering, we had to tie up the tug and the tow in the Seneca River because of high water and a fast current after a prolonged heavy rain storm. While we lay idly waiting for the water and current to subside, I decided to try to rid the tug of the odor and the danger of smouldering wood. I took the valve-cover off our circulating pump and filled the hull of the tug with water above the fire-hold floor. I stopped the pump and let the water lay there for some time and then pumped the bilge dry. This operation put out the fire under the boiler and there was no more smell of smouldering wood the rest of the time I worked on the *Coughlin.* We made two round-trips through the canal which took about five weeks; then the *Coughlin* was tied up in Buffalo, and the crew was laid off due to lack of work. I never worked on the *Coughlin* again, but the next season I was told that she caught fire somewhere along the Barge Canal and was totally destroyed. To this day, I think the fire started under the tug's boiler.

With no further work available with Captain Murphy, I was unemployed for a couple of weeks in July 1935, until I landed a job as second engineer at $120 a month and board on the tug *Metropolitan.* It was fitting out in Tonawanda to do Barge Canal towing. I worked four or five weeks and was again laid off in September due to lack of work for the tug.

The *Metropolitan,* formerly named the *Sylvester Ward,* was built of wood in Boston, Massachusetts, in 1892 and changed owners a number of times before coming under the ownership of a Tonawanda resident. The tug was steam powered, of a good size, and well designed for canal towing but had one bad feature, one that I had never been ship-mates with on a tug. It had rope wheel lines in place of chains or steel cables to operate its hand-powered steering gear. This was a poorly designed, important piece of equipment. The ¾-inch diameter wheel ropes passed through the tug's boiler house, and after a period of time the intense heat dried out the ropes and gradually reduced their strength. Also the sheaves were poorly aligned, and the combination of heat and chafing caused the wheel lines to part under stress. A spare set were always aboard the tug. I had helped to replace a set of frayed steering ropes while fitting out in Tonawanda. An accident to the tug occurred after I had a shore job which was good for the winter, and I did not go back on the *Metropolitan* when the owner secured work towing four molasses barges between Buffalo and Albany.

The barges were heavy built, former New York harbor scows with special steel tanks installed above decks, having sloping bows, and were empty at the time of the accident. The story, as I heard it, was that the tug and four barges were going down the canal a short distance east of the Gasport lift bridge, when a steering rope broke and the tug veered from its course and ran its bow upon the canal bank.

The barges being towed on two short lines ran up and hit the stern of the tug, driving it higher up the canal bank, causing considerable damage to the tug's stern above the water line. Fortunately none of the tug's crew were injured in this serious accident. Although a good part of the tug's stern was under water and leaking after being hit by the barges, the tug's crew was able to keep it pumped out.

Shortly after the accident the diesel tug *Southern Cross,* with a tow of four loaded upbound barges, came in sight and were slowed down to go by the grounded *Metropolitan* and its tow of molasses barges.

At this time the crew of the grounded tug decided to try and use the weight of the passing loaded barges to pull the tug off of the canal bank, by fastening a strong line from the moving barges to the stern towposts of the tug. This resulted in pulling the towposts and most of the stern deck out of the old wooden tug. It then filled with water, sank, and rolled over on its side. The tug was then abandoned to its insurance company who, I believe, abandoned it to the State. The accident happened near the end of the canal season on November 19, 1935. That winter when the canal was empty the State righted the tug, moved it into the empty canal in an upright position and floated it when the canal was filled in the spring of 1936.

The *Metropolitan* was purchased by the Dolomite Company, a Rochester-based firm who repaired and made use of it for a number of years, after which the old wooden steam tug became outmoded by the modern diesel tugs.

I was told that the hull of the old tug was abandoned in a wide-water bone yard in the barge canalized Clyde River a short distance east of Clyde, New York.

CHAPTER 21

The Corps of Engineers

S HORTLY AFTER I turned down Captain Murphy's offer to return to work on the *Coughlin,* an old friend of mine, who had
worked for Cowles as a machinist and who was then working for
the U.S. Army Corps of Engineers, looked me up and told me of a
job he had recommended me for with the Corps. The job, on the
diesel tug *Quintus,* was not much; but it was better and more
secure than the one I had and it paid $90 a month with board pro-
vided when away from Buffalo. The *Quintus* was scheduled to depart for Maine when navigation opened in the spring of 1936. The
tug would be gone six months and the regular deckhand had quit
because he did not want any part of a six months' job in Maine. I
was rather reluctant about it myself, but needed the work and
could see nothing better in the near future. I took the job early
in October and worked as a handyman all winter at the Corps of
Engineers boatyard and repair shop in Buffalo. Not only had the
deckhand quit the *Quintus,* the engineer also quit for the same
reason and it was planned to take the engineer from the Corps'
inspection yacht and put him on the *Quintus* for the trip to Maine.
I was a licensed marine steam-engineer, with some diesel experience while working for Cowles, so I asked for the Chief's job on
the *Quintus.* I was told that the government would hire only
licensed Motor Vessel engineers for their diesel-powered vessels.

Meanwhile, a never-to-be-forgotten family incident took
place that fall on October 20, 1935. Our third child, a son, was

born. My wife's labor began early in the morning. I notified the
doctor and then brought her mother to our house to assist him.
The doctor soon arrived at our home, examined my wife, thought
it would be a couple of hours before the birth took place, and left
to make another call. I don't know if he underestimated the time
or was late in getting back, but the arrival of the baby began without a doctor present. Only her mother and I were there when the
baby was born. The birth was rather slow and the eight-pound boy
was born with a turn of the umbilical cord around his neck. His
grandmother held him up while I untangled the cord. By then, he
had begun to turn blue so I quickly blew into his mouth, then
picked him up by the feet, and slapped him on the butt. He began
to squall and with a sigh of relief I laid him next to his mother
until the doctor arrived a short time later. It was not the custom
then to go to a hospital for childbirth. My wife spent the confine-
ment period at home; my sister looked after her each day until I
returned home from work. The only expense involved was the
doctor's fee of $25, which took me a year to pay.

When I look back on the year 1935, I recall that I had six
different jobs and earned a total of $800 for the whole year.

Before spring came around I took the three-day examination
at the Buffalo United States Steamboat Inspector's Office and
passed a test for a Diesel or Motor Vessel license. I was then
licensed to operate 1,000-horsepower steam or motor vessels and
hoped to eventually become Chief Engineer of the *Quintus.* I was
still the deckhand, however, when the *Quintus* left Buffalo on
May 1, 1936, fully equipped for the trip to Maine, via the Niagara
River, Barge Canal, Hudson River, and then northward up the
Atlantic Coast to Maine. Our destination was Passamaquoddy Bay,
named for a tribe of Indians in that area. It is an inlet of the Bay
of Fundy at the mouth of the St. Croix River, twelve miles long
by six miles wide and shut in by a cluster of islands so as to form
an excellent harbor. The bay is bordered on one side by Maine, on
the other by New Brunswick, Canada. Our assignment was to ferry
around survey crews to map out plans to develop a power project
by harnessing the tides entering and leaving the bay, which has a
tide rise and fall of twenty feet. On our way down the Niagara
River, six miles from Buffalo, our attention was drawn to one of
the Corps trucks sounding its horn on River Road. Pulling in close

to the shoreline we were given this message: "Go back to Buffalo, the Passamaquoddy Project has been abandoned." I never did hear why the project was dropped so suddenly. It was said to be a pet project of President Franklin D. Roosevelt, who spent his summer vacations in that area, on Campobello Island where he had a summer home. The island is not far from Eastport, Maine. Roosevelt was much in favor of developing cheap electric power and at the same time creating jobs for the unemployed during the Depression years.

Shortly after returning to Buffalo, our engineer returned to his job on the Inspector's yacht and I became Chief Engineer on the *Quintus*. I liked the job, and the $60 a month increase in pay was most welcome. It turned out that I spent a pleasant season working for the Corps of Engineers, which, it was said, control a larger fleet of all types of vessels than our Navy. At any rate, a short time after returning to the Corps boatyard, the *Quintus* was put in service towing the derrick boat *Niagara* around Buffalo Harbor, taking care of some routine maintenance work. As soon as this work was finished we were scheduled to leave Buffalo with the *Niagara* to engage in a season's work on Lake Ontario and the St. Lawrence River.

It seems that each winter the ice floes cause debris to lodge in or near the entrance to harbors and dredged navigation channels. That spring, as soon as the ice was clear on Lake Ontario and its harbors, a mobile surveying crew, with portable marine-sounding equipment loaded aboard a large truck, had been sent out from Buffalo. The crew was to measure and sound the depth of water in the harbors and shipping channels on the American side of Lake Ontario and the St. Lawrence River as far as Ogdensburg, New York. Wherever they came across an object that did not allow the required vessel draft, a small buoy or marker was anchored over the spot. A surveyor's transit was then used to pinpoint the spot from location marks on a breakwater wall or the shoreline. A log was kept of each object or shoal spot coming in contact with the sounding boat or sweep. They were called "strikes" by everyone working for the Corps. After the strike and its location was put down in the log, the markers or buoys were removed so they would not interfere with vessel traffic. Some time later the derrick boat arrived to remove the strikes, which were located again with a transit and the log book used by an engineer traveling with the tug and derrick boat. The derrick was equipped with a large clam shell or bucket. The clam shell gripped the strike and lifted it from the water, and the boom swung it to the forward deck of the derrick. When the derrick was finished or had a full load, it was towed out to deep water. The strikes were dumped overboard and were no longer a hazard for boat traffic.

The day soon arrived for our departure to Lake Ontario. We left Buffalo late in June on a fine summer day and had a smooth twenty-mile trip from Buffalo via Lake Erie to Port Colbourne, Ontario. We passed through the Welland Ship Canal that same day and tied up overnight at Port Weller, Ontario, which is now the northern terminus of the canal. The tug and derrick boat were single crewed, and we always tied up after putting in an eight-hour day. The tug crew consisted of a Captain, Chief Engineer, deckhand, and cook. The derrick boat also had a crew of four men.

The next day we went via Lake Ontario to Fort Niagara, where we spent about four days tied up at the mouth of the lower Niagara River, and I recall that I did repair work on the tug's main engine during our stay at the Fort.

My first season spent as engineer on the *Quintus,* which was about five years old at that time, was the first year it had been in service all season without a breakdown. The main engine was a 320-horsepower, 8-cylinder Winton Diesel. It was a chronic fault of the engine to score pistons and bend connecting rods. During our stay at Fort Niagara, I sent a bent connecting rod back to Buffalo to be straightened and installed a new piston and rings along with the straightened connecting rod. The Winton Diesel was a first-class piece of machinery (the manufacturer was bought out by General Motors), and I started searching for the fault which caused these unusual breakdowns. I found the reason and corrected it by a simple adjustment of the external thrust bearing, which had allowed the crankshaft to move too far fore and aft when the direct reversing engine was being maneuvered back and forth.

Our next stop was Rochester, where we spent a few days in the harbor, which is on Lake Ontario at the mouth of the Genesee River. We went on to Sodus Bay, where we removed a number of rocks or strikes from the harbor and the ship channel leading to

The harbor of Little Sodus Bay on Lake Ontario, Fairhaven, N.Y. Center and left is a coal dock which once shipped coal to Canada; to the right is a grain elevator which once received grain from Canada. Note the smokestack and oil-burning headlamp on the locomotive. Tug *E. P. Ross* was the local harbor tug. It was built at Buffalo, N.Y., in 1874 for the Southern Central Railroad Co. of New York. Photo *circa* 1875.

the coal dock, owned by the Pennsylvania Railroad, at the south end of the bay. This was the last coal dock to be kept in operation on Lake Ontario. At one time, I recall, there were three ports on the American side of Lake Ontario that shipped many vessel loads of hard and soft coal to Canada. There once was a large coal dock or trestle at Sodus Bay, which is often called Big Sodus, and another one at Fairhaven or Little Sodus. Oswego was also an important coal-shipping port at one time. The railroads had large coal-storage docks at each of these three ports which were equipped with trestles and made it possible for the coal cars to be pushed atop the storage bins, where the coal was dumped from the cars into the bins. Lake vessels tied up alongside the elevated storage hoppers, chutes were lowered from the trestle, and coal flowed by gravity into the vessels' cargo holds for delivery to Canadian ports. These wooden coal trestles, or docks, began disappearing in the 1930s. They are all gone now, since fuel oil and gas have replaced coal. Today, while there is some commercial shipping from Oswego and Rochester, Big and Little Sodus are used by little else than pleasure craft.

Our next stop with the derrick boat was Fairhaven, where we took some soundings at the entrance to the bay. There was nothing else for us to do here, as the entrance had shallowed out because of sand deposits washed in from the lake. A suction dredge would have to be sent here to remove the sand and restore the required depth. Next, we went to Oswego, where we stayed about a week removing some strikes and taking care of other routine work required in the harbor.

A weekend was a part of our stay in Oswego, for we only worked forty hours a week even while away from our home port. The derrick boat Captain, who also lived in Tonawanda, had brought his car along and had it with him all during that season. He sometimes drove it aboard the derrick boat when we went from place to place, or had one of his crew members drive it for him to the next stop. We had been gone from Buffalo about two weeks when we came to Oswego, and he decided to drive home to visit his family. Chipping in some money for gasoline, four of us went along in his five-passenger Plymouth. We started for home right after quitting time and arrived there Friday evening, spent the weekend at home, and started back for Oswego around 3 A.M., to be in time to begin work on Monday morning. We made such trips every two or three weeks during the season.

From Oswego, we made the forty-four mile run across the eastern end of Lake Ontario without incident to Cape Vincent, which is at the entrance to the St. Lawrence River. We removed a few strikes from the harbor there, and in a couple of days moved on to Clayton and Alexandria Bay, where we cleaned up the work that had been laid out for us at those two river towns.

This was my first visit to the Thousand Island area. It was all new to me and like being on another paid sight-seeing trip. Some of the islands seemed to be no larger than a bushel basket. When we had finished at the bay we went farther down the river to Ogdensburg, a small and pleasant city along the river. We spent about two weeks there doing various small jobs. With not working on weekends, time dragged in a strange town on Saturday and Sunday, but I rode home from the "Burg" only once. This was before the day of the superhighways and the drive to Tonawanda meant a long eight-hour ride each way.

One memorable incident that occurred during our stopover in Ogdensburg concerned a deckhand, who was a former Navy man about 28 years old. He seemed a pleasant-enough fellow, unknown to any of us before he came aboard the tug at Oswego to replace a deckhand who had been called back to Buffalo. The cook confided to me that he suspected the man, who we knew was broke when he came onboard, of stealing money from his shore clothes, which were hung up below deck in our sleeping quarters in the forward end of the tug. The amounts were small, just loose change the cook kept in his pants pocket. But his story reminded me that I, too, had missed a one-dollar bill placed on my locker shelf after leaving Oswego. Since one of the duties of the deckhand was to make up the bunkroom beds each morning, the cook reasoned that that was when the money was disappearing. To test his theory, the cook—in my presence—put some change in the pocket of his pants in the bunkroom. Later that morning, after the deckhand finished his chores in the bunkroom, I checked the trousers and, sure enough, found the pockets empty. We told the Captain, who confronted the alleged thief, and, despite his loud protesting, he was fired—with instructions to return to Buffalo, tell the main office he had quit, and collect what pay he had coming. Though I thought that would be the last time I would see the man. I was flabbergasted the next summer, when I was working for a different marine employer, to see this same seemingly "light-fingered" deckhand working again for the Corps of Engineers as a crewmember on a sounding sweep in Buffalo harbor.

At Ogdensburg the discharged deckhand's place was filled by a man from there, and life aboard the *Quintus* returned to normal, at least for a while.

Although a lot of years have passed since I spent the season of 1936 along Lake Ontario and the St. Lawrence River, I still remember clearly three of the unusual strikes we dredged up at Ogdensburg. The first was a huge water-logged tree trunk; the next was one we did not remove on the first try—a large boulder at least four feet in diameter. It was too big for the derrick boat's clam shell to grip. After lifting and dropping the boulder a few times, it was decided that a diver and his equipment would be trucked down from Buffalo. The diver would go down and fasten a cable around the boulder, which would be shackled to the derrick's most powerful lifting gear. While waiting for the diver and his outfit to arrive, we went about the business of clamming out other strikes that had been buoyed or marked out for us. The next one turned out to be a cast-iron ship's propeller wheel about nine or ten feet in diameter, with the broken end of the shaft still in the hub of the propeller. This strike weighed about a ton and a half, and we put it on the Ogdensburg public dock instead of disposing of it in deep water. The Captain on the derrick contacted a local scrap yard and sold the cast-iron propeller. The derrick lifted the propeller aboard a truck sent down to the dock. The money was divided up amongst the tug and derrick-boat crews, and it amounted to $6 a piece. The extra money was considered a windfall, as most of the crewmen sent their money home and kept only tobacco money between pay days, which was once a month. After disposing of it, I sometimes wondered if the large propeller-wheel with the piece of shaft sheared off at the hub had been broken off by striking the large boulder that we had so much trouble removing from the harbor at Ogdensburg.

The removal of the large boulder was our last job at the "Burg." It was so large and heavy that it could not be lifted above the surface. We towed the derrick to the disposal site with the boulder hanging alongside. The cable attached to it was cut with a torch, and the big stone settled into deep water.

Our next work site was the village of Morristown, twelve miles back upriver from Ogdensburg. A diesel-powered ferry, carrying mostly automobiles, plied the St. Lawrence River between the village and Prescott, Ontario. A small bay on the east shore of the river was the landing place for the ferry, at Morristown. Over the years the bay had shallowed out, making it difficult to maneuver the ferry to its landing place. On our arrival at Morristown, two steel mud dump-scows were there waiting for us, having been brought from Buffalo by another of the Corps tugs, the steam tug *Churchill.* The derrick would keep on loading the empty scow while we towed the loaded one out into the river to dump into deep water outside the ship channel. It was estimated that we would spend six weeks dredging out the harbor.

After working a few weeks at the village, our tug captain was transferred to another of the Corps tugs at Buffalo. A captain living in the area, I believe it was Ogdensburg, by the name of Desar was hired to take his place. He was of French descent, a Great Lakes and St. Lawrence River pilot who knew his business, and he was a good fellow to work with.

About the first of November we finished our work at Morristown and started back for Buffalo with the derrick and the two mud scows. We went as far as Cape Vincent the first day and tied up there for the night. The next day the tug *Churchill* arrived at the cape to assist us back to Buffalo with the tow. We laid there a day or so waiting for good weather before we started across the lake. It was about 10 A.M. on November 3 when the weather had calmed down enough for the *Churchill* to leave the cape for Oswego with the two mud scows. We left soon after with the derrick boat *Niagara*. When about ten miles out in the lake, the captain sent word for me to come up to the pilot house. At that time there was about a fifteen-mile-per-hour breeze and a slight amount of choppy seas which gave a slight roll to our tug and the derrick. When I came in the pilot house he asked me what I thought of the weather. The *Churchill* and her tow were out of sight at this time and must have covered half of the 44 miles to Oswego. I mentioned that I did not think the weather would worsen and that we could keep on going. He said we were near Galloo Island and could find shelter on the lee or sheltered side of the island if need be. Thinking he would keep on going, I gave the matter no more thought and returned to the engine room. A short time later, to my surprise, I received a signal to reduce engine speed. I went on deck, looked around, and saw we were on the lee side of Galloo Island. The captain had decided not to risk the worsening weather and had pulled in back of the island. We let go of our towline and the tug was made fast alongside the derrick scow. There was good water depth around most of the island; this made it possible to push the bow of the derrick scow up to the shore, where a cable was made fast to a nearby tree, and we were prepared to stay there until the wind died down.

I was awakened about midnight; the wind had shifted and we

were being driven onto the island. The tie-up cable was let go and we backed away from the island in a blinding snow storm and headed at slow speed for the other side of the island. In a short time I heard the steel hull of the tug scraping over rocks and had to stop the engine because our propeller wheel was striking them. I thought, "We are in a fine pickle now that we are aground; with it snowing and the wind rising, we could be pounded to pieces." Going on deck, I was relieved to find that we were aground in calm water on the lee side of the island, but it was still snowing. I stepped into the pilot house and asked the captain if I should pump out the tug's ballast tanks in hopes that it would lighten us enough to float the tug. He told me to do so and we were able to back away from the island into deeper water. For the next four hours or so I stayed on watch with the engine running at slow speed while we held the derrick into the wind on the lee side of the island, until daylight.

The weather had turned cold, and when it was light enough we headed for Sackets Harbor. While lying there, I thought about the trouble we had and the time we had lost because we had pulled in for shelter at Galloo Island. The *Churchill* had made it to Oswego, encountering no trouble because of the light breeze, which had held steady all that day. But we laid at Sackets Harbor for two days and did not start out until the *Churchill* came back to assist us to Oswego.

On our way across the lake the captain called me into the pilot house and brought up the subject about some half ship sections that had been towed down the lakes during World War I in 1917. At that time, our government was buying up lake ships to replace vessels that had been sunk, carrying war supplies overseas to Europe. Because the ships were too large to go through the old 250-foot Welland Canal locks, they were cut in two, and a wooden bulkhead was temporarily installed in the open end of each section. Most of the work was done in upper lake ports, though a few of them were prepared in Buffalo.

Tugs towed the half sections down the lakes, through the Welland Canal, over Lake Ontario, and down the St. Lawrence River. They were put together and fitted for salt water operation at Canadian shipyards on the lower St. Lawrence River.

Captain Desar told me of an incident he had been involved

with on Lake Ontario concerning a bow-section of one of the ships. It was late in the fall and he was the pilot on the tug *Tennessee,* which was towing the front half section of the lake vessel *North West.* As they neared the eastern end of Lake Ontario in the middle of the night, they encountered heavy seas and a blinding snow storm.

All was going well on the tug, when suddenly they heard a danger signal from their tow and then heard the faint sound of voices calling for help. They became aware that the temporary wooden bulkhead in the ship was washing out and the vessel was sinking. Thinking it would save time, they untied the towline, threw it overboard, and circled around to take the crew of eight men from the stricken vessel. To their dismay, they were unable to find the ship in the snow storm and could hear the terror-stricken cries of the crew as the vessel sank, drowning all hands. Captain Desar told me, "Had we hauled in the towline instead of throwing it overboard in the snow storm, we might have got back to the tow in time to save the people aboard the ship." He remembered how they were close enough to hear the cries for help, while the tug circled around in the storm trying to find the sinking ship.

The tug had circled around in the area of the sinking until daylight, on the chance that there might be some survivors, but when it became light there was nothing in sight but open water. The *Tennessee* went into Oswego to report the sinking before returning to Buffalo, and since there was no more need for his services as pilot, Captain Desar went home to Ogdensburg.

The loss of the ship's crew had left him with a feeling of guilt he would never forget because of the towline incident. No doubt, it was all brought back to him when we left Cape Vincent on that overcast November day, for we were not too far from the area where that 1917 tragedy took place. Even after going home, the Captain said he was reminded of the sinking each time the local newspaper reported a body had been washed ashore from the sunken ship. As I was about to leave the pilot house, I somehow had the feeling that the Captain was telling me in a roundabout way why he had taken shelter, a few days back, under the lee of Galloo Island.

The two tugs and the derrick boat had a smooth run from Sackets Harbor to Oswego, but there we were weatherbound four days. Meanwhile, Captain Desar did a lot of pacing around the docks while we lay at Oswego, and he looked worried and nervous. I believe it was because we had a lot of late season lake miles to travel before reaching Buffalo. About the third day at Oswego, while we were still waiting for good weather, Captain Desar quit and went home. His nerves had got the best of him and I was quite sure I knew the reason.

Another captain arrived the next day from Buffalo. The following day the weather cleared and we made the run from Oswego to Sodus Bay, where we tied up for the night; then, with two nice days, we made it from Sodus Bay to Rochester. The next day our good weather luck ran out. While lying weatherbound at Rochester, the captain on the *Churchill* had a severe gallstone attack and was sent to a Buffalo hospital. The captain of our tug, the *Quintus,* was put in charge of the tow, and the next morning he stayed in bed with stomach pains! Meanwhile, another captain for the *Churchill* arrived from Buffalo. The next day was calm and sunny; our sick captain was well and on deck, and we made the sixty-mile run from Rochester to Port Weller. We lay there overnight, then went through the Welland Canal, lay in Port Colbourne overnight, and had a good run across Lake Erie to Buffalo the following day.

It had taken us about three weeks to come from Morristown to Buffalo due to the lateness of the season and inclement weather. In mid-season we would have made the run in about six days. That trip took place a long time ago, but I recall we arrived back in Buffalo on November 23, two days before Thanksgiving.

The trip brought clearly to my mind that there is more to being a Captain than just having the title. Captain Desar, as a temporary employee of the Corps, would have been laid off when we arrived at Buffalo. Even though he needed the work, his nerves got the best of him at Oswego, and he quit. The other two captains who became sick after leaving Oswego were steady employees of the Corps. If they had quit, they would have been out of a job in the Depression. I believe their sickness was aggravated and caused by nervous tension. They were responsible for the equipment we were towing, as well as the lives of the crews aboard the tugs and the derrick boat *Niagara.*

It had been a busy season, and even though there were some

anxious moments while scraping the rocks at Galloo Island, there had been no serious mishaps. It had been interesting to visit all the ports on Lake Ontario, the Thousand Islands, and the St. Lawrence River towns. I also learned something of the methods and procedures used to keep the proper depths in the American harbors and shipping channels on the Great Lakes.

CHAPTER 22

End of Log

I SPENT the winter of 1936-37 doing repair and maintenance work on diesel and gasoline engines on various equipment laid up at the Corps Buffalo yard. One of the vessels was a self-propelled suction dredge, a converted former lake vessel used to remove silt and sand from the various harbors and rivers on the Great Lakes. That winter, while working in the shop, I heard the foreman telling the man in charge of the suction dredges of my success with the *Quintus.* I heard the supervisor say, "Garrity would be a good engineer to transfer to one of the suction dredges." That suggestion troubled me. The dredges took care of all the American harbors and rivers on the Great Lakes, carried three crews, and operated twenty-four hours each day, six days a week. The crew's whole off time was spent aboard the dredge, except when they tied up on Sunday. Any of them I might work on may have got to Buffalo during the season and it might not. So, I did not think much of the suggestion, because of the conditions connected with the job.

A short time after fitting the *Quintus* out that spring of 1937, we were towing the derrick boat around Buffalo Harbor, doing some routine maintenance work, when I heard of a two-year tug job that would start that spring on the Mohawk River at Schenectady. It was a union job on a marine contractor's tug, and the wages were twice what I was getting at the time. Still in debt, I had a hard time trying to pay up, on what I was being paid. This fact and the suggested transfer to a suction dredge caused me to quit and take the construction tug job. I was sent with the rest of the crew from Buffalo to Brewerton, New York. The tug had been there all winter, and we finished up some repair work and fitted out the tug. We took a tow of equipment to Schenectady, returned to Buffalo, and picked up more equipment, which we returned again to Schenectady. I sure put my foot in the bucket when I took that job, for on our return we were all laid off. It turned out to be a WPA job and only men from that area were allowed to work on the contract. I returned to Buffalo, mentally kicking myself for quitting the *Quintus*.

Sometime in July I secured a temporary job tallying cords of pulpwood being unloaded from a lake steamer at a local papermill. The tallying job led to a job in what was called the unloading or "bull gang." I helped unload boxcars containing raw materials used in the manufacture of paper. This job almost pulled my cork, but I stuck it out and applied to the personnel man for work in the millwright gang when an opening occurred. Millwrights are all-round mechanics that set up and repair all types of machinery. The work requires a millwright to own a diversified assortment of hand tools. When I began working at the paper mill, it only operated part-time and I never knew, until the weekend, how much time I would get in the following week—one, two, or three days' pay.

During the summer of 1937, working part-time, I was just about able to keep food on the table and a few clothes on our backs. We had three children at this time; we still had a $3,000 mortgage on our home and I was unable to pay even the interest. The mortgage was held by a widow friend of ours. She was a nice person, and I had been acquainted with the lady since I was a boy of thirteen. She called me over one day to tell me that she had to have some money coming in from the mortgage and that if I would pay her $25 a month she would forego the interest and the money would be deducted from the mortgage principal. My wife and I appreciated her generous offer, but we decided that the only way we could make the payments was to move in with my wife's family and rent our own home, which we did. After about a year, I found a small, empty house that was in need of a lot of fixing up to make it livable. I told the owners that I would fix it up if they would furnish the materials and rent it to us. They agreed, and when the house was ready they rented it to us for $8 a month.

Our family looks back on that small place and laughs about it today. The floor in the kitchen was so slanted that our small son used to get on the high side and coast across the floor on his kiddy car. We had only lived in the small house about a month when our fourth child, a girl, was born on January 3, 1939. Another girl was born in 1945 and, in 1947, our sixth and last child, a boy, was born in the house that my wife Mildred and I now live in at Tonawanda. Meanwhile I continued at the papermill until midsummer that year, when I was unexpectedly laid off, but I secured part-time work with the Great Lakes Towing Co. in Buffalo, as a steam tug engineer until the end of the navigation season, when the papermill called me back.

Two years earlier I had taken a civil service examination for a steam fireman's job at the local pumping station or waterworks. In the spring of 1940, I became eligible and took the job as fire man for $1,800 a year. I thought I was all set, as I had job security and a steady income. The job was shift work, mostly shoveling coal and ashes; and, during my second year there I received a week's paid vacation, the first I had ever had. We were slowly getting out of debt and decided we could spend $20 on a short vacation trip that lasted three days. We drove the eighty miles to Chautauqua Lake, a resort area near Jamestown, New York. A night's rent for a tourist cabin cost $2.50, and we ate a good breakfast in a Jamestown department store—bacon, eggs, toast and coffee for twenty-five cents each. The highlight of the trip was seeing and hearing Beatrice Kay sing with a dance band at the resort village of Celeron, which had a large amusement park at that time on Chautauqua Lake. We enjoyed that short vacation, and though we have taken many vacation trips since then, we still discuss that first one.

The economy was beginning to revive in 1941, and I was not too happy with my job at the waterworks. I felt that I had made a step backward and that I was capable of doing something other than shovelling coal and ashes. The British Isles were being bombarded with buzz bombs by Hitler, and the fall of England and the loss of their important munitions plants seemed imminent. The United States was building a number of backup munitions plants, and one was being put in operation that summer in Modeltown, a village about fifteen miles from Tonawanda. Leaving the pumping station, I went to work at the new munitions plant complex as a shift foreman in the water treatment plant. On December 7, 1941, Japan attacked Pearl Harbor, and we were engaged in World War II. Rallied by Churchill and given aid by America, England survived Hitler's bomb attacks. After ten months' employment, the Modeltown munitions plant was shut down as the crisis in England had passed. In the late summer of 1942 I went to work in a wartime shipyard at North Tonawanda that was building LCTs (Landing Craft, Tanks) for the U.S. Navy. After about a year at the shipyard, a steady job as steam tug engineer for the Great Lakes Towing Company opened at Buffalo, and I began working there in October 1943. Of all the jobs I had since my position at Cowles, I liked this one the best. I seemed to be back in my element working on the water, in charge of operating and maintaining machinery.

The Great Lakes Towing Company had harbor tugs in most American ports on the Great Lakes, except those on Lake Ontario. A number of tugs were assigned to each port, and the four-man crews worked eight-hour shifts around the clock. The tugs assisted lake vessels in and out of the harbors. Our range of work covered a waterfront of 36 miles that included the Buffalo and Lackawanna harbors, the Niagara River, and Tonawanda harbor. On occasion I was in a crew that delivered tugs to the company's repair yard in Cleveland, Ohio. We also towed or assisted lake steamers to Port Colbourne, Ontario, and sometimes assisted them through the Welland Canal to Port Weller.

In 1950, the company began converting its fifty steam tugs to diesel power. Having a Motor Vessel license and diesel experience I fitted well into this program. As I think back to this particular time, I had seen and taken part in the transition from animal to steam power, then to diesel power. Today, most tugs and many vessels are propelled by electric power generated by diesel engines.

I enjoyed working for the Towing Company. I worked eight-hour shifts, carried my lunch, and spent my off-time at home. The work and scenery were diversified, the pay was good, and I looked forward to reporting for work each day. I had steady work with the company for twenty-seven years, and retired at age sixty-eight at the end of the 1970 season. The company is still operating in a reduced capacity, but I expect they will be in business as long as lake vessels are running.

Today, I am retired and living with my wife on Social Security and a modest pension earned while working for the Towing Company. I still have some contacts with a few oldtimers that I have known from my boyhood while on my father's canal boats. I am a member of two historical societies and the Canal Society of New York State. What I reminisce about most are the times I spent on the Erie Canal as a young lad, with my brother Jim, a year and a half older than I. Whenever the boats tied up, no matter where, he and I were off and running to find a fishing spot, or to throw stones at mud turtles sunning themselves on logs, and we often discovered and frightened burrowing small animals and snakes which were abundant along the canal and the surrounding countryside. If none of these things amused us, we just roamed about picking and eating fruits or nuts and just taking in the sights.

I never was able to discuss these unforgettable boyhood adventures with Jim in later years; he was a big strapping young fellow when he died at age seventeen, during the 1918 influenza epidemic. Another brother, Robert, drowned in the canal at Tonawanda in 1928, at the age of nine. It seemed ironic that we should lose a member of our family this way, fourteen years after Mother had ceased taking her first seven children on our canal boats. A number of friends and acquaintances who followed the same kind of work as myself, were drowned, and, as I related earlier I was saved from drowning in the canal three times and once fell into deep water but got out safely by myself before I could swim.

Who knows what governs a long or short lifetime? I certainly don't. I sat in church with my father one Sunday when I was fifteen years old, listening to a sermon, and heard the speaker say, "Lead a good life while here on earth, for you are only here a short time." I thought to myself, "Ah, what's he talking about! I could be here another fifty years." Many years have gone by since then, and he was right. It was a short time. Even if I wanted to, I could not change the things that brought me grief or sorrow; but if I had a choice of living my life over again, I think I would begin as the son of the same Erie Canal man that married my mother and always called Liverpool, New York, his hometown.

CANAL BOATMAN

was composed in 11-point IBM Selectric Journal Roman medium and
leaded two points by Metricomp Studios, Inc.;
with display type in Mergenthaler Melior composed by Dix Type Inc.;
printed on 60-lb. Eggshell Cream,
and adhesive bound with paper covers
by Maple-Vail Book Manufacturing Group, Inc.;
with paper covers printed in two colors
by New England Book Components, Inc.;
and published by

SYRACUSE UNIVERSITY PRESS

Syracuse, New York 13244-5160